Country music legend Roy Acuff (right) rose to stardom in the early '40s and was the Grand Ole Opry's leading personality until his death in 1992. An accomplished fiddle player, he promoted the older, classic mountain singing style and resisted modern influences. He is seen here in 1941 with the Smoky Mountain Boys (left to right): Velma Williams, Jesse Easterday, Pete Kirby, Rachel Veach, and Jimmie Riddle.

A TRIBUTE TO THE STARS WHO SHAPED COUNTRY'S GOLDEN AGE

LEGENDS OF
CLASSIC
COUNTRY

TIME
LIFE
BOOKS

A TEHABI BOOK

TEHABI BOOKS

Time-Life Books is a division of Time Life Inc.

TIME LIFE INC.
Chairman and Chief Executive Officer: Jim Nelson
President and Chief Operating Officer: Steven Janas
Senior Executive Vice President and Chief Operations Officer:
   Mary Davis Holt
Senior Vice President and Chief Financial Officer: Christopher Hearing

TIME-LIFE BOOKS
President: Joseph A. Kuna
Vice President, New Markets: Bridget Boel
Group Director, Home and Hearth Markets: Nicholas M. DiMarco
Vice President and Publisher, Time-Life Trade: Neil S. Levin

Staff for *Legends of Classic Country*
Marketing Director: Peter Tardif
NPD Director: Carolyn Clark
Senior Editor: Linda Bellamy
Project Editor: Ruth Goldberg
Director of Design: Kate McConnell
Production Manager: Carolyn Bounds

School and library distribution by Time-Life Education, P.O. Box
85026, Richmond, Virginia 23285-5026.

For information on and a full description of any of the Time-Life
Books series listed above, please call 1-800-621-7026 or write to
Reader Information, Time-Life Customer Service, P.O. Box C-32068,
Richmond, Virginia 23261-2068.

Photography credits appear on page 144.

Tehabi Books designed and produced *Legends of Classic Country*,
and has conceived and published many award-winning books that
are recognized for their strong literary and visual content. Tehabi
works with national and international publishers, corporations,
institutions, and nonprofit groups to identify, develop, and
implement comprehensive publishing programs. The name *Tehabi*
is derived from a Hopi Indian legend and symbolizes the importance
of teamwork. Tehabi Books is located in San Diego, California.
www.tehabi.com

President: Chris Capen
Vice President of Development: Tom Lewis
Design Director: Andy Lewis
Editorial Director: Nancy Cash
Art Director: Vicky Vaughn
Editor: Garrett Brown
Copy Editor: Gail Fink
Photo Researcher: Chris Skinker
Proofreader: Lisa Wolff
Editorial Consultant: Charles McCardell

Library of Congress Cataloging-in-Publication Data

Legends of classic country : a tribute to the stars who shaped
   country's golden age
      p.   cm.
   ISBN 0-7835-5665-9
   1. Singers—United States—Biography. 2. Singers—United
States—Portraits. 3. Country musicians—United States—
Biography. 4. Country musicians—United States—Portraits.

ML400 .L44 2000
781.642'092'273—dc21
[B]   00-062963

The paper used in this publication meets the minimum requirements
of the American National Standard for Information Sciences—
Permanence of Paper for Printed Library Materials, ANSI Z39.48-1984.

Printed by Dai Nippon Printing Co., Ltd., in Hong Kong
10 9 8 7 6 5 4 3 2 1

Front cover: Bill Monroe and the Bluegrass Boys, 1972
Previous page: Johnny Cash, 1972
Opposite page: Hank Williams, c. 1951

CONTENTS

Legends of Classic Country
Pioneers

The man from New York had never heard anything like it. In front of him in a temporary recording studio in Atlanta on June 14, 1923, a fifty-five-year-old mill hand and street musician was scraping out a tune on his fiddle and singing at the same time. The musician was Fiddlin' John Carson; the man from New York was Ralph Peer, who worked for the OKeh record company.

A native of Kansas City, Peer had heard and recorded a good number of vaudeville singers, blues singers, jazz singers, Irish tenors, and opera singers such as Enrico Caruso. But this was something else: one singer, accompanied only by his fiddle, singing in a north Georgian drawl that Peer could barely understand. "I thought it was pluperfect awful," he said later. But he had agreed to make a record of Carson for a local client who promised to buy five hundred copies, and a deal was a deal.

Originally, the Camel Caravan was a network radio show hosted by pop singer Vaughn Monroe, but starting in November 1941 it became a touring road show that traveled to army camps around the country offering free entertainment and free packs of Camel cigarettes. One of the touring groups featured country music, and brought the songs and stars of the emerging genre to thousands of new fans in every corner of the nation. Accordion player Pee Wee King was chosen to lead the troupe, and he performs here with his lead crooner Eddy Arnold (with guitar), a dancer (also with guitar), and singer San Antonio Rose (Eva Nichols). Comedian Minnie Pearl stands to the rear with a mildly disapproving gaze.

Though the Grand Ole Opry went on the NBC network in 1939, it still had many of the qualities of an informal, loosely organized jam session. In this 1940 shot, Roy Acuff bears down on the fiddle, while comic Lonnie "Pap" Wilson (left, with guitar), dobro player Bashful Brother Oswald (a.k.a. Pete Kirby), and Opry founder George D. Hay (with his steamboat whistle) urge him on. The early recording sessions of legendary "artist and repertoire" man Ralph Peer, opposite, gave birth to the new genre that would be called country music.

Peer got back to New York and ordered the record pressed up. One side was an old vaudeville song, "The Little Old Log Cabin in the Lane," that had been written in 1871; the other was an old southern folk tune, "The Old Hen Cackled and the Rooster Is Growing to Crow."

To Peer's surprise, the record became a runaway best-seller. Though southern fiddlers had earlier recorded their tunes on disc, this was the first to feature singing as well, and as a result many historians recognize it as the first country record. It was oddly symbolic, with its two sides representing the two major sources for the early country repertoire: folk songs and old nineteenth-century songs. Within months, every major record company was rushing to get a piece of this new market, scouring the South to find their own versions of Fiddlin' John Carson. The commercial country music industry was born.

Today there are about as many definitions of country music as there are fans. "The name means so much and so little," says Ranger Doug Green of Riders in the Sky. "It is a giant and often neglected tree whose roots into the fertile ground of time and tradition are long and deep and whose branches are many, spreading out broadly to cover a great deal of ground." Singer and songwriter Tom T. Hall once explained, "Country is what you make it," and singer Dolly Parton agrees: "I'm a country person," she reminds everyone. Singer George Jones argues, "I think it's all about love." For Reba McEntire, the music is "blunt and frank . . . When I'm doing country music, I feel like I'm being honest to those people out there." Tammy Wynette offered: "I think little by little we have grown up with our music. We started out with train songs and cotton fields and now we've grown up to the big cities. And I'm sure its gonna change again."

With all the definitions and styles, a few common threads run through each. First, even though not all songs or singers are from rural America or the South, there is always a willingness to pay homage to classic rural values. Even when Tammy Wynette sings so convincingly of divorce, it works because deep down inside her listeners feel that divorce is tragic. Second, the music is generally conservative—both philosophically and musically. Country singers as a rule prefer a small string band ensemble as a setting, and the guitar remains the central instrument—and the key symbol—of the music, just as it has since the days of the Carter Family and Jimmie Rodgers in the '20s. Many singers come out on stage with a guitar even if they don't really play it much; it's just part of what "country is." And finally, though there are dozens of offshoots of country,

ranging from rockabilly to Cajun to "alternative country" and "Americana," there is still a broad central stream of country music that continues to flow like the mighty Mississippi through the center of our culture. This is what we call Classic Country.

About the same time the record companies in the '20s were discovering this new music, radio found it, too. WSB in Atlanta had featured John Carson on the air even before he made his records, and by 1924 WLS, the giant Sears-Roebuck station in Chicago, began a regular program of live country music that became the *National Barn Dance*. The following year, 1925, WSM in Nashville opened, and within weeks had started its own barn dance that eventually grew into the Grand Ole Opry.

With regular live radio broadcasting, more so than with records, early country musicians were able to start making a living with their music. Sponsors like the patent medicine Crazy Water Crystals paid them a semi-living wage, and most stations allowed them to advertise personal appearances in schoolhouses and small-town lodge halls, where they made even better money.

Nobody called it "country" back in those early days. The term most often used was "old-time music," though some records companies called it "old Southern tunes," "old familiar tunes," "native American melodies," or "hill country tunes." For a time in the '30s the northern

record companies used the term "hillbilly" for the music, not realizing that for many southerners the term had racist and derogatory overtones. By the early '40s *Billboard* magazine was calling it "folk tunes" (even though it was quite commercial by then), and the popularity of singing cowboys and western swing bands like that of Bob Wills caused the name "country and western" to emerge in the '50s. By the '60s, with the establishment of Nashville as a center for the music, the term was being shortened to "country."

Once musicians were able to start playing this music full time, it developed with breathtaking speed. It saw its first million-seller in 1925 with "Wreck of the Old '97" by Vernon Dalhart, a formally trained New York studio singer who had a huge appeal to southern audi-

ences. Soon more authentic singers like banjo player Uncle Dave Macon made the scene, singing nineteenth-century folk-derived songs and linking the old vaudeville traditions of the kerosene lantern circuit with the radio and records of the modern age.

From North Carolina came another banjo-playing singer, Charlie Poole, whose "Whitehouse Blues" set the tone for much modern bluegrass. Fiddle bands like the Skillet Lickers (from Georgia), the Hill Billies (from Virginia), and the East Texas Serenaders sold thousands of records. With the discovery—again by

The Delmore Brothers, Rabon (left) and Alton, were among the first great country brother duos of the '30s and one of the most musically sophisticated. Raised in the gospel music tradition in rural Alabama, they joined the Grand Ole Opry in 1933 and soon became one of its most popular acts. They enjoyed a successful recording career, incorporating blues and boogie into their music in the '40s.

Ralph Peer—of the Carter Family and Jimmie Rodgers at a temporary field studio in Bristol, Tennessee, in 1927, classic country vocalists came into their own.

Radio gave birth to a number of early sub-genres of the music. One was the "brother duet" tradition of close-harmony singing, developed by the Delmore Brothers, the Blue Sky Boys, Karl and Harty, and the Monroe Brothers. The high, lonesome sound of bluegrass developed in the late '30s when Bill Monroe put together his first Blue Grass Boys band. Western swing emerged in the Southwest and combined the fiddle band setting with the newer jazz, blues, and swing that bands up north were playing. By the end of the '30s, the success in Hollywood of Gene Autry caused a fad for "western" music, and even those bands from deep within Appalachia were renaming themselves as so-and-so's "Roving Cowboys" and working up versions of "When It's Springtime in the Rockies."

Throughout all of this was also a radio style that featured sweet sentimental songs of an earlier time, and gospel songs old and new; such was the case with Mac and Bob on WLS, with songs like "When the Roses Bloom Again," and Fort Worth's Chuck Wagon Gang, with their "I'll Fly Away."

World War II and its displacements ushered in a new breed of song that dealt more forthrightly with modern problems. The neighborhood bar, the roadhouse, the dance hall, and the honky-tonk became new venues for country music. The old banjo and fiddle gave way to new steel and electric guitars. The older themes of cowboys and roses in May gave way to songs about separation, divorce, drinking, and working. "You Two-Timed Me Once Too Often" sang Tex Ritter in 1945; "Divorce Me C.O.D." echoed Merle Travis in 1946. "One Has My Name, the Other Has My Heart" sang Jimmy Wakely in 1948, while Tex Williams taunted listeners to "Smoke, Smoke, Smoke That Cigarette" (1947). While the pop artists of 1948 were singing about looking over a four-leaf clover and a tree in the meadow, country singers were advising "Don't Rob Another Man's Castle" or reminding us of the sober realities of "The Soldier's Last Letter." It was little wonder that the audience for country was growing all over the land; it was not just good music, but it was relevant music, music you could use.

CHARLES WOLFE

With their familiar string ties and white hats, banjoist Earl Scruggs and singer-guitarist Lester Flatt helped reinvent the old southern string band sound in the mid-'40s. As members of Bill Monroe's band and then with their own Foggy Mountain Boys, they carried bluegrass from the small mountain radio stations and schoolhouse shows to the stage of Carnegie Hall and the studios of Hollywood.

JIMMIE Rodgers

JIMMIE RODGERS WOULD have been vastly amused to learn that history books fifty years after his death refer to him as "the Father of Country Music." In truth, he was anything but fatherly; certainly he was no gray-haired, pipe-smoking, paternalistic, tradition-guarding pillar of the community. He died in 1933 at the young age of thirty-six, after a career that lasted only a little over six years.

Some of Rodgers' hit songs (like "Blue Yodel No. 1" or "T for Texas, T for Tennessee") had elements of older folk songs in them, but many were like nothing that had been heard in country music before—the high, keening falsetto wordless "blue yodels" that became his trademark. Though many of his songs relied on Victorian rhetoric (like "Daddy and Home" and "Treasures Untold"), others dealt with two-timing women, pistol-packing ladies, boozing, and getting thrown in jail. He sometimes sang with only his acoustic guitar, but just as often experimented with all kinds of pop music backups, ranging from Hawaiian guitars to Louis Armstrong's jazz trumpet to a New York string studio orchestra.

Jimmie Rodgers not only sold records to coal miners and farmers, but also traveled to Hollywood and toured the major vaudeville stages. He absolutely dominated the fledgling country music scene of the '20s, when his popularity easily rivaled that of Garth Brooks in the '90s. Rodgers was the model for generations of later singers, from Gene Autry to Ernest Tubb, from Hank Snow to Lefty Frizzell, from Tanya Tucker to Merle Haggard.

Rodgers did not come from the southern mountains, but from the rolling flatlands of southern Mississippi, where he was born in the railroad junction of Meridian in 1897. The area was a hotbed of delta blues singing, and while young Rodgers absorbed some of this, he spent

With his trademark western hat and his brand-new customized Weymann guitar, "America's Blue Yodeler" strums a chord in 1928. Rodgers' career was on an upswing. During the next five years, he toured many cities nationwide and recorded more than 100 titles. While Rodgers' success was cut short in 1932 by the Depression and his own declining health, he will forever be remembered for his quintessentially American music. As inscribed on his statue in Meridian, Mississippi: "His was an America of glistening rails, thundering boxcars, and rain-swept night, of lonesome prairies, great mountains, and a high blue sky."

Both Jimmie Rodgers and comedian and writer Will Rogers were at the peak of their fame when they toured the Southwest on a Red Cross benefit tour in the winter of 1931. The comedian would die in 1935 in a plane crash with aviator Wiley Post.

the first dozen years of his young manhood traveling around the country working on the railroad, often as a brakeman. Contracting tuberculosis in 1924, he turned to singing, and in 1927 talked his way into an audition for the Victor Talking Machine Company at a temporary studio in Bristol, Tennessee. A lackluster record resulted, but four months later Rodgers appeared unannounced at the Victor headquarters in Camden, New Jersey, wanting to record again. This time he unleashed his famous "Blue Yodel," and it became one of music's first genuine million sellers. His Victor "artist and repertoire" (A & R) man, Ralph Peer, was amazed with his potential, and took over as his manager.

During the next five years, Rodgers recorded some 110 titles, including a whole series of "Blue Yodels." Critics of the time didn't know what to make of him—one reviewer dubbed him "White Man Gone Black"— but fans did, and bought his records by the carload: "Away Out on the Mountain," "In the Jailhouse Now," "My Old Pal," "Waiting for a Train," "Hobo Bill's Last Ride."

In 1929, Rodgers went to Hollywood to make a short film called *The Singing Brakeman,* and in 1931 he toured with famous comedian Will Rogers, who called him "my distant son." The deepening depression, however, ravaged his record sales, and his worsening health made it more and more difficult to tour.

In May 1933 he traveled to New York for a final session. By this time he was so weak he had to rest between recordings, but managed to finish a last set, concluding with a song called "Years Ago." He died two days later, on May 26. His death brought forth a wave of tribute songs from other young singers who had modeled their work after his, and his records continued to sell throughout the '30s. Indeed, many of them have remained constantly in print in the seven decades since his death, and still sell strongly today on compact disc.

Jimmie Rodgers was the first great country singer, the first performer inducted into the Country Hall of Fame, and he helped establish the genre of country music as a viable entity on the commercial music scene. "My time ain't long," he said in one of his songs, but he used that time as effectively as any singer before or since.

CHARLES WOLFE

Though he made only one short film, Rodgers often presented himself on stage as a singing cowboy, and many of his best songs dealt with western themes. Below, in his famous "ice cream" suit, he is shown with country's other superstar act of the era, the Carter Family, at a recording session in Louisville in 1931.

The CARTER Family

Even when people all over the country were buying their records, the Carters continued to live and work on their farmsteads in the remote Poor Valley in southwestern Virginia. A. P. Carter, his wife Sara (right), and her cousin Maybelle (left) spent as much of their time in aprons and work clothes as in performing garb.

THE DISCOVERY OF the Carter Family is probably the best known and most written about legend in country music history. It took place in the sleepy mountain town of Bristol, whose Main Street formed the state line between Virginia and Tennessee, in the late summer of 1927.

It was a Monday evening about dusk, and standing in a temporary studio set up by the Victor Talking Machine Company were three people from the hamlet of Maces Spring, Virginia: a lean, intense 36-year-old man named A. P. Carter, his wife Sara, and her cousin Maybelle Addington Carter. They were poor people, plainly dressed, who had borrowed a car to drive over dirt roads to get to the town. Maybelle played the guitar, Sara played a mountain instrument called the autoharp, and all three sang. They began their session by doing an old folk song they had known all their lives, "The Storms Are on the Ocean."

Ralph Peer, the A & R man in charge of the session, at once knew he had something special. "As soon as I heard Sara's voice," he recalled years later, "that was it. I knew it was going to be wonderful."

It was. Within a matter of months, Carter Family records were selling all over the South, and everybody was singing Carter Family songs like "Keep on the Sunny Side" and "Anchored in Love." Maybelle's distinctive guitar playing, Sara's lead singing, and A. P.'s ability to find good songs made them the archetypal country singing group. They brought harmony to the music, and translated the old Appalachian folk music into the style of country and bluegrass. They created dozens of songs that became standards in these fields and major influences on artists as diverse as Woody Guthrie, Johnny Cash, Bill Monroe, Emmylou Harris, Vince Gill,

In his later years, A. P. Carter assumed the role of a genial country storekeeper and grandfather—though he lived to see some of his songs re-popularized by young groups like the Kingston Trio. In this 1959 photograph taken at his home in Hiltons, Virginia, he entertains four of his grandchildren, Rita, Dale, Lisa, and Connie.

and Doc Watson. They would also start a dynasty of later Carters that would continue up until the present time.

The Carters came from Poor Valley, nestled between towering Clinch Mountain to the north and the Holston River to the south. A. P. (Alvin Pleasant) Carter was born there on December 15, 1891, to a family that had been in the valley since Revolutionary War times. He met Sara Dougherty in 1914, when he hiked over the mountain trying to peddle fruit trees; the first time he saw her she was playing the autoharp and singing "Engine 143." They were married in 1915, and began singing at local churches and schoolhouses. It wasn't until 1927 that they were joined by Sara's teen-aged cousin Maybelle.

The Carters soon became one of Victor's best-selling artists, second only to Jimmie Rodgers. Over the next fourteen years, they recorded more than three hundred titles for virtually all the major labels of the day, and mastered a wide variety of material, including folk, gospel, Victorian parlor, topical ballads, blues, cowboy, sentimental, and even comic songs. Their best known songs, many of which they recorded several times, included "Wildwood Flower," "Little Darling Pal of Mine," "John Hardy Was a Desperate Little Man," "Will the Circle Be Unbroken," "Gold Watch and Chain,"

"Wabash Cannonball," "Cannonball Blues," "I'm Thinking Tonight of My Blue Eyes," "Worried Man Blues," and "Lonesome Valley."

Unlike their counterpart Jimmie Rodgers, the Carter Family never successfully worked the big-time vaudeville circuit, but they did work widely in radio in the '30s. Their tenure on the so-called "border stations" in Del Rio, Texas, gave a huge boost to their record sales and fan mail.

Though A. P. and Sara separated in 1932, they continued to tour and record together until Sara retired in 1943. A. P. and Sara, accompanied by their children, made a brief comeback in the early '50s, recording for a small Kentucky label named Acme. A. P. died in 1960, just at the start of the folk music revival that would rediscover his music.

Maybelle built a new act with her daughters Helen, June, and Anita and worked for years on shows like the Old Dominion Barn Dance and the Grand Ole Opry. June later married Johnny Cash, and Mother Maybelle and the girls often toured in the '60s as part of his show. Sara even joined Maybelle for a brief comeback and reunion album in 1967.

Today an amazing number of the old Carter albums are still in print on CD, and an impressive number of Carter songs survive as standards with new generations of country singers. Maybelle's "Carter scratch" on the guitar is one of the first skills a beginning guitar player learns. The Carter style that was born long ago in that makeshift studio has become a cornerstone for all of country music.

CHARLES WOLFE

The Carters defined the family singing group as a genre of country music, and established a dynasty that continues even today. The rare informal shot below reflects the gentle give-and-take of a family gathering, while the center image shows a '50s incarnation of the group with Sara, A. P., and their daughter Janette (right).

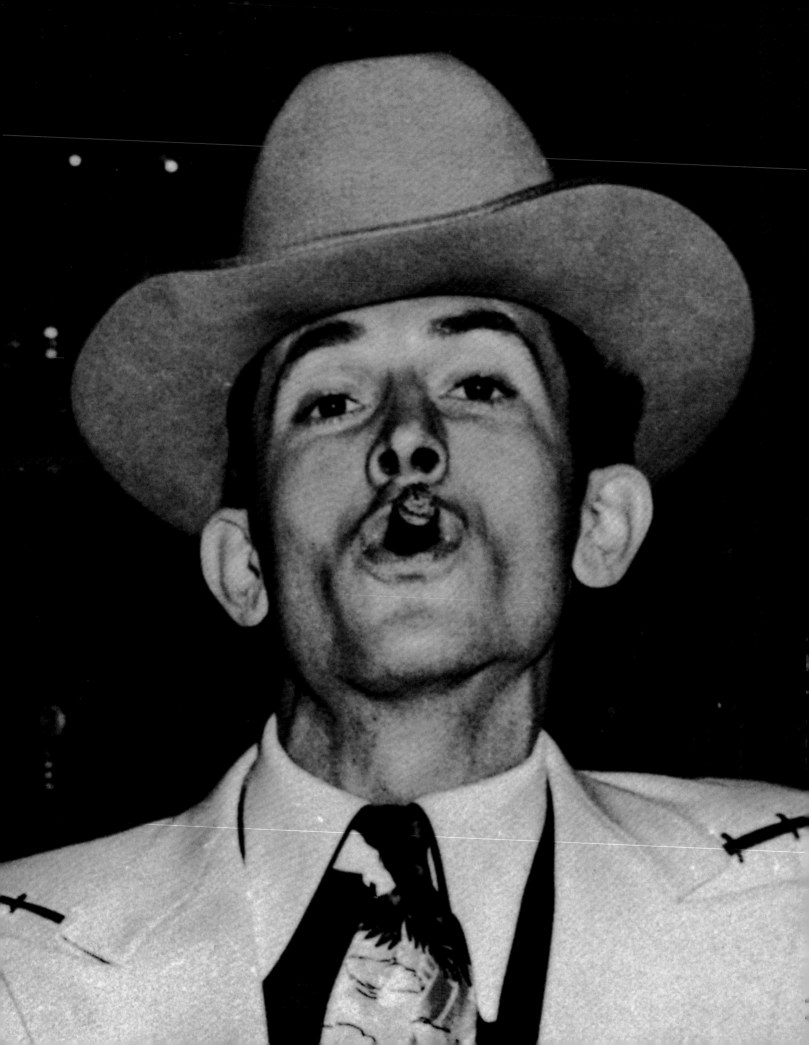

HANK Williams

HANK WILLIAMS IS, without contest, the most powerfully iconic figure in country music—iconic to the point that man and myth are inextricably entwined. He set the standard for contemporary country songcraft and sang his songs with such believability that, although gone for nearly half a century, he still seems very real to us. His brief life and tragic death have only compounded his appeal.

Soon after Hank's death, the little truths in his songs became reduced to clichés, and those clichés were pounced upon by those who disliked country music. Honky tonkin' and cheatin' hearts. So easy to parody. Williams' songs were desperately real when he sang them, though. Little sonograms of life, certainly his life. A deeper study of his work reveals a haunted spirituality. Hank once sang of being pursued by the "Pale Horse and His Rider," and when he directly addressed "The Angel of Death"

in song, he could bring a chill to any room. He sang as if he had just seen a video of the rest of his life.

Billboard magazine discovered the essence of Hank Williams in its review of his first record in February 1947: "With real spiritual qualities in his pipes, singing with the quality of a camp town meeting, Hank Williams makes his bow an auspicious one." How right they were. That "real spiritual quality" was present in all his work, the hymns in particular.

Hank Williams' star appeared to rise fast, but he'd served a ten-year apprenticeship by the time he scored his first hit, "Move It on Over," in 1947. He was twenty-three then, and twenty-five when the overwhelming success of "Lovesick Blues" (a song he did not write) earned him an invitation to join the Grand Ole Opry. Three years later, he had been dismissed from the Opry, and four months after that he was dead. Williams had just

Hank Williams, shown here on an Opry tour of Germany in 1949, flaunted his success at a time when other country artists wore humility as if it were a crown of thorns. His arrogance often infuriated his fellow performers, although few would concede as much after his death, and his natural cockiness often escalated when he was drinking, which further alienated many of his peers.

Publicly, Hank Williams wore two faces: the charismatic performer and the devoted family man. Performer Williams appears at the Opry (background) with Chet Atkins (to his right) and at the Riverside Rancho in Los Angeles with fiddler Jerry Rivers and steel guitarist Don Helms. The family man poses at home in Nashville with first wife Audrey, infant son Randall Hank, and Audrey's daughter, Lycrecia.

six years as a recording artist, and during that time, recorded only sixty-six songs under his own name—plus a few more as part of a doomed husband-and-wife act, Hank and Audrey, along with a number of others under his moralistic alter ego, Luke the Drifter. Of the sixty-six songs recorded under his own name, though, an astonishing thirty-seven were hits. More than once, he cut three songs that became standards in one afternoon. His natural voice, an unassuming baritone, could be shaded in a seemingly infinite number of ways, echoing the sentiments of his songs.

The fourteen "Luke the Drifter" recordings were mostly narrations. Luke the Drifter walked with Hank Williams and talked through him. If Hank could be headstrong and willful, a backslider and a reprobate, then Luke the Drifter was compassionate and moralistic, capable of dispensing all the sage advice that Hank Williams ignored. Luke the Drifter had seen it all, yet could still be moved to tears by a chance encounter on his travels.

As a songwriter, Hank Williams matured surprisingly quickly, and his fractious relationship with Audrey provided him with all the raw material he needed. His songs found a wider market after Tony Bennett covered "Cold, Cold Heart," and from that point there was a rush to reinterpret his songs for the pop market. Ironically, those versions, which comfortably outsold Hank's own in the early '50s, now sound dated, while the spare and haunting originals sound ageless.

Contrary to myth, Hank did not die with his star in the ascendant. "Jambalaya" was one of the top-selling records of 1952, but while his records were topping the charts, he was so unreliable that he was reduced to playing beer halls in Texas. There's a persistent assumption that he would have returned to the Opry had he not died on New Year's Day 1953, but surviving correspondence suggests nothing more than a few more beer hall gigs.

Timing is everything and Hank Williams came and went at precisely the right time. Country music was a cottage industry just a few years before his arrival, yet, just a few years after his death, it was shaking off its "hillbilly" image, and an artist as unapologetically rural as Hank Williams would have been shown the door. Elvis Presley appeared on the Grand Ole Opry just two years after Hank was dismissed, and Nashville's response was to find other artists who could cross between country and pop. Hank Williams didn't belong in that world, and his early death spared him the indignity of trying. Instead, he and his music remain remarkably untainted by compromise, and he remains the most mythical figure in country music.

COLIN ESCOTT

The classic lineup of Hank Williams' Drifting Cowboys featured Howard Watts on bass, Jerry Rivers on fiddle (standing next to Hank Williams), Sammy Pruett on guitar, and Don Helms on steel guitar. The stripped-to-basics sound perfectly complemented Williams' raw emotionalism.

Ernest TUBB

By the time "the cowboy came to Nashville," Ernest Tubb had jukebox record hits and bit parts in two B-western Charles Starrett movies. He brought his western look and honky-tonk sound to WSM, Nashville, and its Grand Ole Opry in 1943. The Texas-born singer-songwriter enjoyed a long, successful career during which he helped many younger artists achieve stardom. He was the longest-touring country performer, giving 150 to 200 shows each year from the early '60s until illness forced his retirement in 1982.

ONE OF THE earliest honky-tonk country singers is Ernest Tubb. He was the prototypical singer-songwriter and the composer of all of his best early material. He and his music were products of their time and place—in his case, Texas of the '30s and early '40s.

A pioneer of the direct and explicit musical treatment of heartbreak, drink, and alienation later known as honky-tonk, Tubb reached that style by way of the music of America's "Blue Yodeler," Jimmie Rodgers, and cowboy music. Most of his Texas contemporaries and fellow honky-tonk pioneers (Cliff Bruner, Ted Daffan, and Floyd Tillman) came there from western swing backgrounds. But by 1946, Tubb's mix of these two elements, with certain personal touches, made him the jukebox market's biggest star. His voice had already dropped to the low registers in which it stayed, and he sang with a drawl, exuding a warmth that some compared to an audible smile. His voice wore well on his listeners, not grating, and could be taken in large doses. It was so distinctive and recognizable that it begged to be imitated, and often was.

In part because he lived the life he sang about (more perhaps than he might have liked), Tubb had a sincerity that was unmistakable. Mrs. Jimmie Rodgers helped him in his early days because she heard in Tubb that believability—a quality that never deserted him over a career of five decades.

Tubb not only could sing, but wrote great songs as well. Before his muse deserted him in the late '40s and he turned to material from other songwriters, Tubb by age thirty-five had written most of his career hits—his signature song "Walking the Floor Over You" and so many others that spoke to his beloved World War II generation, like "Blue Eyed

Tubb's genial Decca Records labelmate Red Foley hosted the Grand Ole Opry's network half-hour between 1946 and 1953. The two friends joke around behind a Decca microphone placed on the Opry's stage in 1949, just before making their first of some twenty recorded duets.

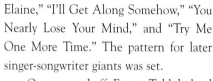

Elaine," "I'll Get Along Somehow," "You Nearly Lose Your Mind," and "Try Me One More Time." The pattern for later singer-songwriter giants was set.

Onstage and off, Ernest Tubb helped establish the traditionally close rapport between a country music star and his fans. He took his concerts seriously, presenting them with dignity and professionalism, demanding the same of his band and fellow artists, and he signed autographs or posed for pictures as long as it took to satisfy all present.

Behind the scenes, that same brand of generosity led him to do more than anyone else for aspiring or deserving young country singers. He eventually prospered through the growth of his Ernest Tubb Record Shop in Nashville, but he started it at the peak of his fame more as a service to fans in far-flung places who couldn't find country records; because of it, many a country singer's record royalty checks were a little larger. Soon *Midnight Jamboree*, the late-night radio show from that record shop, blanketed the country on Sunday mornings right after the Grand Ole Opry and became a talent showcase for hopeful artists like Patsy Cline, Loretta Lynn, and countless others.

Songs Tubb didn't choose to record he often pitched to those he felt could do them justice; a classic case was his insistence that Ray Price record Bill Anderson's "City Lights." Young Stonewall Jackson and other artists in need of a helping hand got tour dates with Tubb. He helped bring Hank Williams and Hank Snow to the Grand Ole Opry, he helped keep the Wilburn Brothers on the Opry, and out of his own Texas Troubadours band nurtured two stars of the '60s and '70s, Jack Greene and Cal Smith.

In sum, Ernest Tubb's career hallmarks were three closely related characteristics—sincerity, integrity, and longevity. He believed in what he was doing, so much so that he never wanted to retire or do anything else, and that came across in his music. His integrity could almost be heard as he sang: once he found his style, he saw no reason to change it, sell out, or reinvent himself.

That integrity, along with Tubb's physical stamina, perseverance, economic need, and loyal fans, explain his longevity to some extent, but the fact that he kept singing his old songs in his old way made him new generations of fans as swings in the stylistic pendulum brought him back into vogue. It happened to Tubb twice—during his '60s career resurgence ("Be Better To Your Baby," "Thanks a Lot," "Waltz Across Texas") and his final performing years (1978–1982), when, busy as ever on the road, he became an oft-quoted and deservedly oft-honored elder statesman of country music.

RONNIE PUGH

Tubb's move to Nashville led to the creation of his band, the Texas Troubadours (the 1945 version surrounds the touring car), and he simply wouldn't do concerts, broadcasts (like this 1972 CMA Awards telecast), or recording sessions without them. After 1947 Tubb also had a record shop to operate (brand-new when he and first wife Elaine posed in front), so the singer and businessman had little time left for publicity stunts like this '50s baseball swing with a guitar.

BILL Monroe

THERE'S A COMMON joke told at bluegrass festivals about a man who dies and goes to heaven. An angel is showing him around. "That's the pearly gate over there, and that's Saint Peter with the keys. And up here's the street of gold." The newcomer notices a stately white-bearded man in a robe carrying what appears to be a mandolin. "Who's that?" he asks. His host replies, "That's God. He thinks He's Bill Monroe."

Such almost sacrilegious awe was common to Bill Monroe. For years his fans have considered his work the sacred texts of bluegrass music. Fans have named their children after him, and left untouched instruments he had tuned or played. Where country fans feel free to refer to their heroes as "Hank" or "Willie" or "Merle," bluegrass fans still refer to their patriarch as "Mr. Monroe."

For most of his career, Bill Monroe was a daunting presence who didn't like

pandering to the public or giving interviews to the press. He was a complex, enigmatic artist for whom his music and his individuality were more important than his image or his show business success. "I've always thought my music would speak for itself," he once said, and over the years, it has. He is the only figure in country music—and one of the few figures in American culture—who has actually invented a musical style. When people call him "the Father of Bluegrass," they are literally correct.

Though bluegrass has often been associated with the Appalachian mountains, Monroe was born and grew up in the hills of western Kentucky, not far from the Ohio River, in the community of Rosine. There he first heard the elements he would later forge into his new music: the square dance fiddle tunes of his Uncle Pendleton "Pen" Vandiver, the gospel singing of the old rural shape-note

Bluegrass was born in Bill Monroe's mandolin as much as in his high, lonesome singing. A superb technician and a driving innovator, Monroe composed dozens of instrumentals on the mandolin, and even worked out the leads to his vocal numbers on his hallowed Gibson F-5. Monroe rejuvenated older country sounds during a profile career that spanned five decades. Among the diverse artists he influenced were Elvis Presley, George Jones, and the Everly Brothers.

As a young man, Monroe got his first professional job in music as a square dancer for the National Barn Dance touring show in the '30s, and he often broke into an old-time buck dance on stage in later years. Here he does an impromptu turn with a clogger from the bluegrass show at Nashville's Fan Fair in 1979.

singing schools, the old ballads of his mother, the blues of neighbors like black guitarist Arnold Shultz, and local string bands like the Prairie Ramblers.

By 1934 Bill and his older brother Charlie had formed a guitar-mandolin team and were singing on the radio professionally; after they moved to North Carolina they began recording for Bluebird, and on the strength of their hit "What Would You Give in Exchange for Your Soul?" soon became the most popular duet act in country music.

After the brothers split up in 1938, Bill formed his own band, calling it the Blue Grass Boys after the nickname of his home state; in 1939 he won a slot on the Grand Ole Opry by singing a version of "Muleskinner Blues" that featured his own sky-high tenor.

In 1946 he hired banjoist Earl Scruggs and singer Lester Flatt, and his bluegrass sound was complete; Scruggs' revolutionary three-finger style electrified Opry audiences, and Flatt's warm baritone formed a perfect lead to Monroe's tenor. In an age of honky-tonk songs and increasingly electric instruments, Monroe maintained his original acoustic sound

and featured sentimental songs like "Blue Moon of Kentucky." In 1950 he began a long association with Decca, and created many of his "true" (i.e., autobiographical) songs such as "Uncle Pen," "My Little Georgia Rose," "I'm on My Way to the Old Home," and "In Despair."

After suffering through hard times in the '50s, Monroe found a huge new audience in the '60s with the rising folk music revival and the emerging bluegrass festival scene. In addition to his traditional southern fans, Monroe now appealed to college students and young white-collar urbanites. He continued to develop his music and for a time carried three fiddlers in his band. He created new instrumental masterworks like "Scotland," "Wheel Hoss," and "Jerusalem Ridge." After a cancer scare in the early '80s, Monroe responded by writing the haunting mandolin solo "My Last Days on Earth." All told, he recorded over five hundred pieces during his career.

When he died in 1996, his funeral was held in Nashville's Ryman Auditorium, former home of the Opry. Fellow performers Ralph Stanley, Ricky Skaggs, Vince Gill, and Marty Stuart paid a musical tribute that proved his legacy was in good hands.

CHARLES WOLFE

The future and past of bluegrass are captured in these two images. At left, Monroe teams with his protégé Ricky Skaggs, at Monroe's home in 1982. Below, an early incarnation of the Blue Grass Boys from 1940 features Art Wooten on fiddle, Cleo Davis on guitar, and Amos Garen on bass.

Roy ACUFF

Showman Roy Acuff, with Howard "Howdy" Forrester diligently fiddling away beside him, wows a Grand Ole Opry audience with one of his signature stunts—balancing his bow and fiddle on his chin, a holdover from his days as a medicine-show busker. Similar antics earned Acuff's band the nickname the "Crazy Tennesseans" during their early days.

FOR THE LAST twenty years before his death in 1992, Roy Acuff spent most of his time as the living legend in residence of Nashville's Grand Ole Opry. He seldom toured, recorded little of consequence, and wrote no new songs; he presided as patriarch and spokesman for the Opry and, by extension, for country music in general, appearing each week on the show to sing his signature song "The Wabash Cannonball" and welcoming tourists to Opryland USA, the show's theme park.

The Opry management even built him a little house just across from the entrance to the new Opry House, provided a home for his museum, named a smaller theater after him, and, in later years, commissioned a sculpture of him and his old friend Minnie Pearl to grace the lobby of the renovated Ryman Auditorium. His presence on the Nashville music scene was inescapable,

and tourists who got into country music through Garth Brooks or Shania Twain well might wonder just what Acuff had done to deserve all this.

As always, timing had a lot to do with it. Acuff came to the Opry in 1938, just a year before the show went on the NBC network and gained a truly national audience. He immediately emerged as the most popular performer on the network portion of the show, and his appeal helped sell the show to the network audience. In many ways, Roy Acuff founded the Nashville music scene.

As his band name suggested, Acuff really was a Smoky Mountain Boy. Born in the east Tennessee town of Maynardsville in 1903, Acuff grew up listening to rural neighbors sing the old lonesome ballads, and his grandfather play the old fiddle tunes. After a severe sunstroke cut short his career as a baseball player, Roy took up the fiddle and by

Very much a family man, Acuff fools around on the fiddle with his only son, Roy Neal, in the late '40s. By the mid-'60s, Roy Neal had indeed followed in his father's footsteps, and actually had a handful of chart hits before he decided to leave music and turn to painting.

the early '30s was good enough to perform on local Knoxville radio stations. Gradually he also began to sing, and in 1936 came across an old gospel song called "The Great Speckled Bird." It became his most requested number, and eventually won him a recording contract and a job on the Opry.

The '40s was Acuff's greatest decade: monster record hits; Hollywood films; huge tour audiences; and even a run for the governor's office in Tennessee.

Unlike so many performers in the '40s, Acuff never adopted the western style and music of the singing cowboys; he steadfastly refused to dress his band in cowboy garb, though Hollywood pressured him to, and he kept alive on the Opry the older, classic mountain singing style—a soulful, emotional, high-pitched "straining" style that was especially effective on sentimental and gospel songs.

His big record hits included "The Precious Jewel" and "Wreck on the Highway" (1940), "Fireball Mail" (1942), "Wait for the Light to Shine" (1944), and "Two Different Worlds" and "Blue Eyes Crying in the Rain" (1945). On many of these, he was accompanied by "Bashful Brother Oswald" (Pete Kirby), one of the first to popularize the dobro (resonator guitar) as a backup instrument and one of

the great tenor singers of the time. And all this happened at the very time the Opry, and Nashville, emerged into the spotlight as the center of the commercial country music industry.

In 1942 Acuff went into partnership with Fred Rose, a veteran songwriter who had started out writing pop songs and jazz in Chicago and cowboy songs for Gene Autry. The pair formed Acuff-Rose Publications, which laid the foundation for the country music publishing empire in Nashville, and in later years numbered among its writers Hank Williams, Redd Stewart and Pee Wee King ("The Tennessee Waltz"), the Louvin Brothers, Don Gibson, Felice and Boudleaux Bryant ("Rocky Top"), and Roy Orbison. By 1985 the company controlled some 20,000 copyrights.

Highlights of Acuff's later years included his 1962 induction as the first living member of the Country Music Hall of Fame and his participation in the 1971 landmark album *Will the Circle Be Unbroken* with the Nitty Gritty Dirt Band. He continued to be a staunch defender of the older, more traditional styles of country music and took seriously the nickname bestowed on him years before by baseball great Dizzy Dean, "The King of Country Music."

CHARLES WOLFE

Roy Acuff's performing years spanned five different decades. In the '40s, one of his many Opry tour groups included (from left) legendary banjoist and singer Uncle Dave Macon (standing) and his son Dorris, famed dobro player Bashful Brother Oswald, and, blowing his trademark steamboat whistle, Opry founder George D. Hay; kneeling are three other members of the Smoky Mountain Boys, Lonnie "Pap" Wilson, Jess Easterday, and Rachel Veach. In a 1949 shot (probably on tour in Germany), Acuff signs photos for GIs. And at an '80s backstage gathering at the Opry, Roy shares a laugh with his protégé Boxcar Willie (right) and longtime comedy partner Minnie Pearl.

Forever associated with the rise of Flatt & Scruggs was their longtime sponsor, Martha White Flour, with "hot rize." On tour, the Foggy Mountain Boys would often give away free sacks of the flour, and the advertising jingle the boys devised for it became so popular that they finally had to record it.

FLATT & Scruggs

WHEN LESTER FLATT and Earl Scruggs left the big-time Opry band of Bill Monroe in 1948 to strike out on their own, it was, recalls Scruggs, "like walking into a strange room with the lights off." At first they took their new band, the Foggy Mountain Boys, into a succession of smaller radio stations in the Appalachians—at Bristol, Roanoke, Knoxville, and Versailles, Kentucky, and were signed to a new, smaller record label, Mercury.

Yet to many fans of the new bluegrass music, Lester Flatt's warm, lazy baritone and trademark guitar runs on the lower strings and Earl Scruggs' dynamic, three-finger banjo playing were some of the qualities that best defined the genre. On the Opry, announcer George D. Hay had introduced Earl as "that boy from North Carolina who can make the banjo talk," and the Opry crowd would explode into shouts and applause when Earl finished a solo. Now every young banjo player in the

South was trying to figure out how to master the smooth three-finger roll they heard Scruggs playing.

Like Monroe, Earl Scruggs did not come from the mountains; he was a flat-lander, born in 1924 in Flint Hill, North Carolina. He developed his rapid-fire banjo technique as a teenager, basing it on the work of older local players. Lester Flatt, who was born in the Tennessee mountain village of Sparta, grew up working in textile mills and playing guitar with radio bands—including that of Bill Monroe's brother, Charlie. Flatt and Scruggs met in 1945 when both joined Bill's band.

Though the Foggy Mountain Boys didn't actually have many chart hits— bluegrass bands seldom do—they produced in the '50s a body of classic recordings that, with Monroe's work, pretty much defined bluegrass. Their catalog included "Foggy Mountain Breakdown,"

"Salty Dog Blues," "'Tis Sweet to Be Remembered," "Don't Get Above Your Raisin'," "Blue Ridge Cabin Home," "Rollin' in My Sweet Baby's Arms," "Why Did You Wander?" and other songs that soon won them a place on WSM Nashville, a spot on the Opry, and a famous sponsor (Martha White Flour).

But their national break came in 1962, when they were picked to do the theme song for the popular new CBS-TV series *The Beverly Hillbillies;* in fact, their music was so popular that in later episodes Lester and Earl were written into the script, playing themselves as old friends of the Clampetts. Even more fame came in 1967, when "Foggy Mountain Breakdown" was used as theme music for the block-buster film *Bonnie and Clyde.* By this time, it was Flatt & Scruggs, not Bill Monroe, who for millions of Americans came to symbolize bluegrass.

CHARLES WOLFE

By the '60s, Josh Graves (center) had added his dobro to the sound of the Foggy Mountain Boys, and often he, Scruggs (left), and bass player Jake Tullock added their voices to Flatt's (right), especially on gospel songs.

EDDY Arnold

With his boyish good looks and easygoing style, young Eddy Arnold became an early matinee idol as he rose to fame in the late '40s. Though he later favored blazers and tuxedos, his first image was that of the folksy "Tennessee Plowboy." Arnold's early success included a string of Top Ten recordings, appearances at the Grand Ole Opry, and the Camel Caravan tour of military bases.

EVEN IF HE had not been one of the smoothest stylists in country music history, even if he had not taken the music into venues like Carnegie Hall, even if he had not pioneered singing in supper clubs in a tuxedo, Eddy Arnold would have a place in the record books.

Like a baseball Hall of Famer, his statistics are impressive. The *Billboard* files show him with a total of 145 best-selling singles and total record sales in excess of 85 million, making him one of the biggest-selling country stars of all time. Arnold holds the records for the Most Top Ten Hits (92), the Most Consecutive Top Ten Hits (67, between 1945 and 1956), and the Most Weeks at the No. 1 Position (145). If he were playing in the majors, his lifetime batting average would be over .400.

Unlike those of so many singers who came up during the '40s, Eddy Arnold's career didn't peak, or ebb and flow; his appeal spanned the generations, and as late as 1966, when most singers from his era were resting on their laurels, Arnold was voted Favorite Male Vocalist on the strength of his No. 1 hit the previous year, "Make the World Go Away." He was also that year voted into the Country Music Hall of Fame. Soon he was taking his career to even newer heights, mounting stage shows at Lake Tahoe, doing television specials with Perry Como, dancing on the *Tonight* show with Ginger Rogers, attending a state dinner at the White House with Lyndon Johnson.

Long before the "crossover" phenomenon was common in the industry, Arnold's records routinely danced up the pop charts. His easygoing singing style made him the first of the great country crooners—a line that runs from Jim Reeves to Kenny Rogers. Few singers have had careers as long or distinctive,

An early family portrait captures Arnold with wife Sally and daughter Jo Ann.

and fewer still have created a style so instantly recognizable.

Not bad for a boy who grew up in a family of sharecroppers in the flat farmland around Henderson in west Tennessee. Born in 1918, the young singer saw his father die on Eddy's eleventh birthday, and his family watched as their farm was auctioned off to pay debts. "I was just existing, not living," Eddy recalled of his poverty. "The only way I knew how to change it was through singing." At seventeen, he decided to give it a try. "I just lit out," he said.

After radio jobs in Jackson, Tennessee, and St. Louis, Eddy got a job with Pee Wee King on the Grand Ole Opry in 1940. He gained wide exposure singing with King on the NBC network, and then later with the Camel Caravan, a touring group that visited army bases around the country. By 1943 he was ready to go out on his own, and in 1945 had his first chart hit, "Each Minute Seems a Million Years."

Arnold soon found the perfect instrumental backing for his singing—the steel guitar of Nashville native Little Roy Wiggins. At a time when the electric non-pedal steel was still a noisy and exotic instrument, Wiggins figured out how to play with the sweet, achingly pure "ting-a-ling" sound that made the steel the favorite backup sound of the '50s. Arnold-Wiggins classics tumbled forth: "I'll Hold You in My Heart," "It's a Sin," "Bouquet of Roses," "Don't Rob Another Man's Castle," "Anytime." The year 1955 saw the recording of "The Cattle Call," the old cowboy waltz that would become Arnold's theme.

The end of the '90s saw Eddy Arnold retired from the supper club circuit, but still recording an occasional album. Wise investments made him one of the wealthiest performers in Nashville, and as he looked back over his career, he had good cause to reflect on the truth of the title of his autobiography: *It's a Long Way from Chester County.*

CHARLES WOLFE

To thousands of later fans, Arnold was known as "Eddy the Crooner." He is shown, at the left, onstage at a Cleveland, Ohio, event called Musicarnival. For years Arnold was closely associated with Checkerboard Jamboree, the national radio shows he did on the Mutual network for the Ralston Purina company in the late '40s. Even in more recent years, Arnold has never lost his handsome looks and winning smile.

BOB Wills

FEW MUSICIANS HAVE been associated with one form of music as completely as Bob Wills has been with western swing, that uniquely depression-era form of Southwestern jazz played on country string instruments. The Texas fiddler may not have been the first such bandleader, but he was far and away the most prominent and most enduring.

Born in east Texas in 1905 but raised on a west Texas farm, Wills first made his mark playing with the Light Crust Doughboys in Fort Worth in 1930. Singer Milton Brown left that band in 1932 to form the first western swing band, with Wills doing likewise the next year. Bob Wills and His Texas Playboys took shape while broadcasting regularly on KVOO and playing weekly dances at Cain's Academy, both in Tulsa. They first recorded in 1935. But these skeletal facts barely hint at the extraordinary story.

Wills' music was unprecedented: at the height of the Jazz Age, he surrounded the traditional country string band style with jazz and pop musicians like pianist Al Stricklin, as well as country pickers like steel guitarist Leon McAuliffe. With Smokey Dacus on drums—then unheard of in a string band—Wills played dances exclusively. His unprecedented combination of jazz and country was scorned and mocked by many traditional country and "legit" music fans alike. But he ruled Texas—which was heir to a melting pot of American music styles—and then the West.

Wills' repertoire reputedly grew to 3,600 songs, including ancient fiddle tunes, square dances, commercial country, waltzes, boogie woogie, blackface and minstrel style, gospel, cowboy songs, polkas, blues, New Orleans jazz, two-steps, schottisches, Tin Pan Alley pop, classical, Mexican songs, and more. Though he himself remained a straightforward country

He defined his musical turf before World War II, but Bob Wills later expanded on the sound while "going Hollywood" with his horse Punkin. Bob Wills and His Texas Playboys (he based the band in California after his 1943 army discharge) made fifteen western movies between 1940 and 1946. On personal appearances, they replaced their original English-cut suits with western duds.

Wills wanted the best of both worlds. Though a country breakdown fiddler himself, he was a consummate bandleader with an ear for hot-jazz sidemen. The Texas Playboys swung with style and substance alike.

fiddler, he paired himself against "hot" fiddlers like Jesse Ashlock, and added brass and reeds, ultimately putting two front lines—one of fiddles, one of horns—onstage in front of the rhythm section. They improvised solos like the citified jazz greats.

Directed by guitarist-arranger Eldon Shamblin, Wills' bands grew to twenty-two pieces and, played songs like "Big Beaver" with as much polish and drive as the era's top orchestras. But they also remained funky and down to earth. The Playboys also captured Wills' sound on record with the infectious spontaneity they displayed live, resulting in a remarkable body of work that's still being reissued and learned by new bands today.

Wills introduced original tunes like "San Antonio Rose" and "Faded Love" that have become standards. The Playboys dressed in stylish, western-cut suits that exuded class, defying the popular image of country musicians as "hicks." And Wills had tremendous charisma, directing the band onstage with fiddle in hand and cigar in mouth, letting fly with his trademark "A-ha!" cry of pleasure when the music so moved him. In an era when the farmers and

country folk who made up his core audience were struggling just to squeak by, Wills seemed bigger than life. But through it all, he projected the humble, just-folks image that allowed his fans to look at him almost as family, and as the personification of their own most valuable traits and dreams.

The original Texas Playboys were torn apart by World War II. After the war, the music spread across the Southwest to California, where Wills himself lived for several years, fronting new bands and appearing in movies.

As his career dried up in the '50s and '60s while Nashville solidified its hold on country music, he turned to smaller groups and reverted to his earliest, most traditional, sound. But before Wills died in by 1975, he'd seen Merle Haggard revive his name and sound with a 1970 tribute album, followed by a 1974 Playboys reunion set. Wills was also the spiritual forefather of the '70s "Outlaw" movement led by Willie Nelson. Today, Asleep at the Wheel is the most prominent band to carry the torch for western swing; in Texas, dancehalls remain popular and Bob Wills is still the King of Western Swing.

JOHN MORTHLAND

The maverick Texan often battled the Nashville industry, forcing drums onto the Grand Ole Opry and helping popularize amplification. But he glowed while being inducted into the Country Music Hall of Fame by Tex Ritter (center) and Roy Acuff (right) in 1968.

The elements of Gene Autry's classic singing cowboy image were all in place even before he left the Midwest for Hollywood in the mid-'30s: the white hat, custom guitar, tailored shirt, and fancy boots. To kids, it was cool; to parents, it was safe.

GENE Autry

UNLIKE SO MANY of the white-hatted knights who galloped across the silver screen, Gene Autry was a singer first and a cowboy second. Though many remember him today as the two-gun hero riding Champion and singing "Back in the Saddle Again," or as the proprietor of the radio favorite *Melody Ranch*, or as a pioneer in making children's records like "Rudolph the Red-Nosed Reindeer" and "Peter Cottontail," or even as the owner of the Los Angeles Angels, Gene Autry was an absolutely top-notch singer.

Before he first set foot on a Hollywood sound stage (in 1934), Autry had proved himself as a serious interpreter of white blues, a capable imitator of Jimmie Rodgers, a purveyor of cowboy songs like "The Last Roundup," a singer of protest songs like "The Death of Mother Jones," and the owner of the huge hit record of the sentimental classic "That Silver-Haired Daddy of Mine."

For some seven decades, Gene Autry was a fixture on the American pop culture scene, and, along the way, one of the biggest record sellers in country music. He was the first country singer to show that there is a dramatic tie between media exposure and record sales.

Born in the small Texas ranch town of Tioga in 1907, Orvon Gene Autry appeared to be destined for a career as a railroad telegrapher when he met by chance one day the famed humorist Will Rogers. Rogers heard Autry singing and advised him to go to New York to try his luck; he used one of his free railroad passes, made the trip, and landed contracts with several companies in 1929.

Autry's next stop was the WLS *National Barn Dance* in Chicago; the powerhouse station was owned by Sears and Roebuck, and soon the ubiquitous Sears catalogues were featuring Gene Autry Roundup guitars and Gene Autry Conqueror Victrola records.

After a casual trip to Hollywood, the singer made his first feature film in 1935 with *Tumblin' Tumbleweeds*. By the end of the decade, Gene Autry was ensconced as America's leading singing cowboy, and throughout America families who would never let their children listen to "hillbilly" music were eagerly buying tickets to see "clean Gene" at the Saturday matinee.

The '40s saw a long line of Columbia hits like "Mexicali Rose," "Ole Faithful," "Amapola," the wartime anthem "At Mail Call Today," and the Christmas favorite "Here Comes Santa Claus." Autry's warm, relaxed singing style had, like that of Bing Crosby, become one of the most recognized sounds in American music.

CHARLES WOLFE

From 1940 to 1956, Wrigley chewing gum sponsored Autry in one of the longest-running radio shows, *Melody Ranch,* whose popularity rivaled his films. Even so, by the start of World War II Autry was voted the fourth most popular movie star, one of the reasons he joined with Shirley Temple (right) to urge fans to buy more war bonds.

Legends of Classic Country
1950s

To borrow a line from Charles Dickens, the 1950s were the best of times and the worst of times. The front end of the decade saw the rise of country's two greatest singing stylists, Hank Williams and Lefty Frizzell; the latter part saw the ascent of rock 'n' roll and its devastating effect on country music record sales and concerts. "They came that close to killing off country music in the '50s," recalls singer Johnnie Wright. It was a time when singers such as Tony Bennett and Rosemary Clooney had hits with pop versions of great Hank Williams songs like "Cold, Cold Heart," and yet was an age when such hard-edged honky-tonk singers as Webb Pierce made new converts, and when the new sound of the pedal steel guitar cried from the jukeboxes of a thousand taverns.

This era was the time when modern country music as most people know it today was born. At the start of the

Two of the singers who defined the decade, Ray Price (left) and Ernest Tubb (second from left), discuss a song with pop singer Tony Bennett, while Jack Drake (right) looks on. It was Bennett's pop recording of Hank Williams songs in the early '50s that helped convince New York that Nashville songsmiths could compete with the best of them. And in later years, Price, who initially followed a hard-core honky-tonk path, would himself add strings and lush arrangements to his own records.

Webb Pierce was one of country music's top stars during the '50s, with thirteen singles topping the *Billboard* charts. His distinctive singing style made him one of the most popular performers of the honky-tonk era. Pierce recorded his ninety-sixth and last record in 1982. Rose Maddox, opposite, emerged as a star with her family's band, the Maddox Brothers & Rose, in the late '30s. She launched a solo career two decades later, and in the '60s became the first woman to record a bluegrass album.

decade, *Billboard* listed the ten best-sellers (unlike later, when they would list the "hot 100") of what they were now calling "country and western records." This was when Nashville came into its own as the music's capital, when the major record companies decided to open offices there, when the Grand Ole Opry solidified its base as the nation's leading country radio show, when the songwriting system jelled and fell into place, when women artists emerged as more than window dressing for the road shows, when record producers began to use a cadre of gifted studio musicians who devoted most of their time to working in studios, and when people started calling Nashville "Music City."

The dramatic changes of the '50s can be seen by looking at the progression of hit records. The first big hit of the decade was "Chattanoogie Shoe Shine Boy" by forty-year-old Red Foley. Though a native of eastern Kentucky, Foley was very much a '40s-styled singer whose warm, smooth, unaccented voice was closer to Bing Crosby's than Hank Williams'. Foley had come to fame on Chicago's *National Barn Dance* and then moved to Nashville to replace Roy Acuff on the network portion of the Grand Ole Opry in 1946; by 1955 he had moved

to Springfield, Missouri's, pioneering TV show *Ozark Jubilee*, bringing with him standards like "Old Shep," "Peace in the Valley," and "Mississippi." His "Chattanoogie Shoe Shine Boy" was a cute song with slightly racist overtones that had little in common with the hardcore drinking songs that soon replaced it on the charts, such as Hank Williams' "Long Gone Lonesome Blues."

After Lefty and Hank broke the ground with their songs about drinking, despair, loneliness, betrayal, and lost love, other young singers followed, ushering in the golden age of honky-tonk music. The new crop included east Tennessee native Carl Smith, Texan and western swing figure Hank Thompson, fellow Texas singer Ray Price, the Washington, D.C., bar singer Buzz Busby, west coast singer Skeets McDonald, and the handsome part-time movie star and singer Faron Young.

In 1953 Webb Pierce created one of the greatest drinking songs, "There Stands the Glass," a song so convincing it was banned from some radio stations. His 1954 classic "Slowly," with the famous introduction by studio musician Bud Isaacs, helped establish the pedal steel guitar as a fixture in the music. Born in West Monroe, Louisiana in 1921, Pierce was one of the charter members of KWKH's *Louisiana Hayride* before he joined the Grand Ole Opry in 1952. Through the decade, Pierce's high, hard, nasal voice graced some thirteen No. 1 hits, more than either Lefty or Hank. His Nashville lifestyle included his famous guitar-shaped swimming pool and his co-founding of Cedarwood Music, a major publishing company.

Following in the steps of Kitty Wells, whose 1952 hit "It Wasn't God Who Made Honky-Tonk Angels" opened the door for modern country songs from a woman's point of view, came major figures like Jean Shepard, an Oklahoma native whose "Dear John Letter" became her career song; Rose Maddox, who with her brothers galvanized the west coast with her boisterous, unpredictable performing style; and the remarkable Charline Arthur, whose sense of independence and determination to call her own shots caused her to clash with the male-dominated industry and eventually led to the collapse of her career.

In 1956, the rock 'n' roll revolution hit country full force; those younger singers, like Marty Robbins, who could adapt to the new sounds did so and flourished; those who could not, or would not, went through lean times. Oddly, in the early days it was country that helped nourish rock 'n' roll. Elvis Presley did his first big-time tours on package shows with Hank Snow, Kitty Wells, and Faron Young. Popular radio shows like the *Louisiana Hayride* and *Big D Jamboree* encouraged as much rockabilly music as straight country. Independent record companies like Sun, Starday, and King routinely released country next to rock 'n' roll, and had no

problems with younger country singers adding drums to their sessions.

Rock 'n' roll didn't go away, as some predicted (and hoped) it would. But by the end of the decade, a new nationwide fad for folk music renewed interest in the classic country style, and gave the faltering industry a much-needed shot in the arm. The last big hits of the decade included Johnny Horton's saga song "The Battle of New Orleans," Johnny Cash's cowboy ballad "Don't Take Your Guns to Town," and the Browns' "The Three Bells," based on a French folk melody.

Country music had met the challenge of the new music and the youth revival, and had survived with its identity intact. It had laid the foundation for the next generation.

CHARLES WOLFE

RAY Price

Ray Price started out in the early '50s as a musical disciple of Hank Williams—singing and dressing like him and even borrowing his Drifting Cowboys band after Williams' death. Before long, however, Price began crafting his own sound, which gradually evolved from hardcore honky tonk to fluid western shuffle to light jazz and finally to the burnished "countrypolitan" pop of "Danny Boy" and "For the Good Times."

WHETHER MOANING HONKY-TONK blues or purring an intimate love song, Ray Price has set dauntingly high standards. To appreciate his musical reach, one need only listen to his tradition-centered first hit, "Talk to Your Heart," move on to the earnest shuffle of "City Lights" and the jazzy offhandedness of "Night Life," and then go directly to his sonorous, lavishly orchestrated "For the Good Times."

In his earliest singles, like "Road of No Return" and "Talk to Your Heart," Price affected the pinched-throat delivery and semi-yodel flourishes of Hank Williams (albeit without the hard nasalizing). As Price developed his own style, he eased into a lower vocal range, relying more on slashing fiddles and weeping steels for emotional intensity. By the time he arrived at "For the Good Times," he was displaying the warm, vibrant baritone and chiseled enunciation of a classic pop singer.

Although Hank Williams' influence is apparent, Price seems to have been marked just as deeply by the great crooners of his youth—Bing Crosby, Frank Sinatra, Nat King Cole, and Perry Como. Born January 12, 1926, near Perryville, Texas, Ray Noble Price came of age in a world far less musically fragmented than it is now. Radio was still the big news then, and even small stations boasted an invigorating mixture of locally grown and network-carried sounds—everything from rural string bands to romantic pop warblers to symphony orchestras. Paving the way for Price were the likes of Eddy Arnold, Red Foley, and Tennessee Ernie Ford, middle-of-the-roaders who regularly commuted between hillbilly and the mainstream balladeer sound.

Price's musical apprenticeship was brief. After serving in the marines from 1944 to 1946, he enrolled at North Texas

Before he moved on to tuxedos and a magisterial stage presence, Ray Price was the easygoing "Cherokee Cowboy," with all the western duds and folksy mannerisms to match. He joined the Grand Ole Opry in 1952, where he shared the stage with such renowned artists as comedian Minnie Pearl, left, and singer-actor Curly Ray Sanders, below, who opened for him in the late '50s.

Agricultural College, intending to become a veterinarian. Instead, he began performing around campus and eventually dropped out of school. In 1948, he made his radio debut in Abilene, where he began billing himself as "The Cherokee Cowboy." The next year, he progressed to the *Big D Jamboree* in Dallas. After recording one single for Dallas-based Bullet Records, Price signed with Columbia in 1951.

While still in Texas, Price fell under the artistic sway of Hank Williams. In Nashville, the two became close friends and, for a while, roommates. After Williams died, Price hired his band, the Drifting Cowboys. Later editions of Price's stellar bands included Roger Miller, Willie Nelson, Johnny Paycheck, and Johnny Bush.

To the degree that Price mimicked Williams' style, he did it well and soon progressed beyond it. The song that gave Price his own musical identity came in 1956. Sweeping in on a wave of fiddle and a propulsive 4/4 shuffle beat, "Crazy Arms" shot to No. 1 and stayed there for twenty weeks. The next year, his "My Shoes Keep Walking Back to You" crossed into the pop charts. He would have nine more pop crossovers, the loftiest being "For the Good Times," which went to No. 11.

Price notched his second most durable hit in 1958 with "City Lights," a thirteen-week chart-topper. With *Night Life* (1963), the dark reverie written by his sideman Willie Nelson, Price displayed his gift for jazz, phrasing the lyrics to his own dramatic clock, even as his musicians ground out the mechanically even up-front dance beat. As early as 1965, with "The Other Woman" and "Don't You Ever Get Tired of Hurting Me," Price was edging into his smooth, urbane ballad stage. He boldly drove this point home in 1967 with "Danny Boy," a song whose majestic string backing alienated many of his old fans.

For the Good Times (1970) re-energized Price's career. Besides its crossover success, it earned him a Grammy for best country vocal performance and set him up for three more No. 1 singles: "I Won't Mention It Again" (1971), "She's Got to Be a Saint" (1972), and "You're the Best Thing That Ever Happened to Me" (1973). His last of 109 charted country singles came in 1989 with "Love Me Down to Size."

At the age of seventy, Price was elected to the Country Music Hall of Fame in 1996, an award that was long overdue. He had modernized the honky-tonk sound with the "Ray Price Beat" in the late '50s, and greeted the year 2000 as more of a pop singer, still elegant and in superb voice.

EDWARD MORRIS

More than just a versatile vocal stylist, Price has also been a trendsetting bandleader. This hand-picked ensemble backing him on an Opry appearance in 1961 illustrates the key elements of his early honky-tonk style—keening twin fiddles, a pulsating bass, and high, urgent vocal harmonies.

KITTY Wells

ONE OF THE many people who listened to Kitty Wells in the '50s was Kentucky singer and songwriter Tom T. Hall. He wrote: "Kitty was the first lady to come out and tell her side of the story about honky-tonks and cheating and those kinds of things . . . the harsh realities of life. Like every other country boy and girl, I thought she was phenomenal. I was fascinated by her music and was interested to hear the other side of the story as told by the ladies."

Hall was not alone in his love of her music. The body of records Kitty Wells produced from 1949 to 1957 were unparalleled in country music history; they defined, in essence, the role of women in modern country music, and opened up the classic honky-tonk style of Hank Williams and Lefty Frizzell to new perspectives. They contained frank new statements about divorce, loneliness, unfaithfulness, and drinking that brought the music into line with the realities of modern working-class life. And audiences responded: at one point, Kitty Wells records remained in the Top Ten for 161 straight weeks. She worked at earning her title, "the Queen of Country Music."

Before Kitty Wells the only other major female soloist in country music had been Patsy Montana, who back in 1935 had sold millions singing about a Never-Never Land of white-hatted cowboys and their sweethearts in "I Want to Be a Cowboy's Sweetheart." Kitty's signature song, "It Wasn't God Who Made Honky-Tonk Angels" (1952), with its famous line "Too many times married men think they're still single," pretty much put the cowgirl image to rest.

And yet there was never a less likely revolutionary than Kitty Wells. Actually born in Nashville—a rarity in country circles—Muriel Deason grew up singing in the local Nazarene church and on

Decked out in full skirt, frills, and gingham, and looking very much like the young mother and busy wife that she was, Kitty Wells in the early '50s was making the dramatic transition from singing old-time gospel and sentimental songs like "I'll Be All Smiles Tonight" to the newer honky-tonk hits like "There's Poison in Your Heart."

By the '60s, the Kitty Wells—Johnnie Wright touring troupe had become a family affair, with daughter Ruby and son Bill joining the show and establishing careers of their own.

Nashville radio WSIX with her two sisters and a cousin. In 1937, when she was eighteen, she married a young singer named Johnnie Wright and spent the next decade raising a family and singing part-time with his radio band. The group wandered from station to station and while at Knoxville, Muriel Deason Wright became Kitty Wells. "Johnnie picked the name from an old folk song they used to sing on the Grand Ole Opry," she recalls.

By 1952 Johnnie had teamed with Jack Anglin to form a new act called Johnnie and Jack, and they soon had a major hit record, "Poison Love." With a steady income from the duo, Kitty decided it was time to retire and tend to their growing family. But then Decca's Paul Cohen talked her into recording an "answer song" to Hank Thompson's "The Wild Side of Life," which had been a big hit. She was lukewarm about the new song, about "honky-tonk angels," but finally agreed to record it. She recalls, "I said, 'Well, it probably won't make a hit, but we will at least get a session fee out of it.'" She got her check for $125 union scale and returned home. It was only a few weeks later that she ran into Audrey Williams, Hank's wife, who told her, "Honey, you've got a hit on your hands."

Decca was now eager to tap into this new market, and encouraged Johnnie to find the best new songs tailored for Kitty's style. A string of masterpieces followed in the '50s: "Paying for That Back Street Affair," "Making Believe," "Lonely Side of Town," "Amigo's Guitar." Kitty's delicate, haunting voice, framed by the classic steel guitar and fiddle, spoke to generations. Duets with Webb Pierce and Red Foley anticipated future duets by Conway Twitty and Loretta Lynn. Kitty continued to have chart hits well into the '70s, and managed more than a hundred tour dates a year into the '90s. She was elected to the Country Music Hall of Fame in 1976, and was presented with the Grammy's Lifetime Achievement Award in 1991.

CHARLES WOLFE

Until his tragic death in a 1963 automobile crash, Johnnie Wright's brother-in-law Jack Anglin (below right) worked as his duet partner in the wildly popular act Johnnie and Jack. For much of her early career, Wells worked with them, and many of her hits came from the pens of her husband and Anglin. At left, an honest-to-goodness native of Nashville, Wells is all smiles with her mother, Myrtle Deason.

LEFTY
Frizzell

Lefty Frizzell exploded onto the scene in 1950 with the release of his two-sided smash, "If You've Got the Money, I've Got the Time" paired with "I Love You A Thousand Ways," Frizzell originals that would provide another pretty fair Texas songwriter, Willie Nelson, with chart hits in the late-'70s. Lefty, who drew from the styles of Jimmie Rodgers and Ernest Tubb, in turn influenced George Jones, Merle Haggard, and Willie Nelson by showing how honky-tonk music should be sung. Lefty Frizzell was only twenty-two years old when his first records hit big, and his boyish charm and Texas smile attracted girls the way Elvis Presley would in later years.

IN THE FALL of 1951 the two hottest acts in country music, Hank Williams and Lefty Frizzell, ran into each other at the Key Club in Printer's Alley in Nashville. Williams had been having hit records since 1947; Frizzell was a newcomer making his entrance in a spectacular way: that fall he had four records in the Top Ten, a feat never accomplished before or since.

Hank walked up to Lefty's table, sat down, and looked at the tall, young, boy-faced singer in front of him. In a kidding way, he said, "Here, boy, why don't you just stay down in Texas? This is my territory up here." Lefty smiled and said, "Hank, the whole damn country is the back yard for both of us. Can't you realize there's enough room for all of us?" Hank grinned back. "Actually, it's good to have a little competition. And boy, you're the best competition I ever had."

The two singers soon became friends, and for a time actually shared a dressing room at the Grand Ole Opry. And though Hank's career would soon end in tragedy, and Lefty's would fall on hard times, the two would emerge as the two most influential stylists in modern country music. Hank represented the old higher-pitched honky-tonk style, while Lefty embraced a softer, more soulful sound in which he would break a syllable into three or four notes and "snake" the melody through a song. It is Lefty's style that is heard today in the work of his followers like Merle Haggard, Randy Travis, Buck Owens, and Keith Whitley. Lefty once said, "When I sing, every word has a feeling about it. I had to linger. Had to hold it. I want to hold one word through a whole line of melody. I didn't want to let go of that no more than I wanted to let go of the woman I loved."

Born in Corsicana, Texas, William Orville Frizzell grew up in the rough-and-tumble oil fields of east Texas and

There was no mistaking Frizzell's custom guitar, as seen in this shot from a radio show in the '50s. During this decade, he recorded numerous Top Ten hits and toured extensively.

Louisiana. He got the nickname "Lefty" in a schoolyard fight when he was a boy; since he played the guitar with his right hand, the used his left to knock out a school bully. (His record company would later insist he got the name as a Golden Glove boxer.)

As a boy, Lefty would hold his head inside the old Victrola horn and listen to the yodeling of Jimmie Rodgers. By 1947, when he was nineteen, he was married and had his own radio show in Roswell, New Mexico. A statutory rape conviction led to a jail sentence, during which he wrote to his wife what would become one of his best-known songs, "I Love You a Thousand Ways." For a time, he returned to the oil fields, but in 1950 met Jim Beck, the owner of a Dallas recording studio who also served as a talent scout for Columbia Records.

Beck got Lefty a contract on the basis of a song Lefty had written called "If You've Got the Money I've Got the Time." It launched the young singer's career, and within months was followed by other mega-hits like "Always Late" and "Mom and Dad's Waltz."

From 1950 to 1953, the singer had thirteen Top Ten hits, and seemed poised to take over the throne vacated by Hank Williams' death in 1953. But a series of bad management decisions, drinking problems, and simple bad luck dogged Frizzell, and by 1954 he had abandoned his southwest base for a relocation to California. He had no major hits until "Long Black Veil" in 1959, and in 1962 he moved to Nashville, where he had his last major hit with "Saginaw, Michigan" in 1964.

In later years, Lefty wrote a lot with Whitey Shafer, producing such masterpieces as "That's the Way Love Goes," which became a No. 1 hit for Merle Haggard in 1983. He continued to make great records, even though his former commercial success eluded him. On July 19, 1975, he suffered a massive stroke, and died soon after; he was only forty-seven. His friend Merle Haggard, who had devoted an album to Lefty's songs, summed up his influence by saying Lefty was "the most unique thing that ever happened to country music." Thousands of fans, and hundreds of singers, agreed.

Charles Wolfe

Though he seldom used any cowboy or western songs in his music, Frizzell found it hard to turn his back on his southwestern upbringing, as witnessed here with his custom-made buckskin jacket and Roy Rogers–styled bandanna.

Johnny CASH

JOHNNY CASH'S INIMITABLE sound came lean and crisp out of the cotton fields of rural Arkansas, his voice a rumbling, primal instrument pushed along by the chicka-chicka rhythms of his own acoustic guitar, the music punctuated with twangy single-note, electric guitar runs from Luther Perkins and supported by Marshall Grant slapping out a percussive foundation on string bass.

Whether beseeching a porter to alert him at the glorious moment when the train he rides crosses into his native Southland; hanging his head and crying at the sound of a train whistle, tortured by the thought that others go free while he rots in Folsom Prison; or keeping a close watch on his heart, his eyes wide open to his commitment to be true in a relationship, Cash sounds impassioned and unique, at once a voice of the people and set apart from everyone.

"We were just a plain ol' hillbilly band with a plain ol' country style," the Man in Black sings in "Luther Played the Boogie," a 1955 recording for Sam Phillips and his Memphis-based label, Sun Records. Elvis Presley came first at Sun, but Cash and his band, the Tennessee Two, had a style all their own, far from plain. Three years in Memphis, working with Phillips, yielded recordings as diverse as the up-tempo rock 'n' roll number "Get Rhythm," the mournful "Home of the Blues," the folk-based "Rock Island Line," and the sugary pop tune "Ballad of a Teenage Queen."

In 1958 Cash moved to Columbia Records and, for a time, to California. By the early '60s he was exploring themes in concept albums including *Ride This Train* (1960); *Blood, Sweat, and Tears* (1962); *Bitter Tears: Ballads of the American Indian* (1964), and *Ballads of the True West* (1965). Embraced as part of the folk music revival, Cash sang about western

Johnny Cash dressed in black to identify with "the poor and the beaten down," he explained in the song, "Man in Black." Shown here on January 14, 1970, hosting his ABC-TV show at Nashville's Ryman Auditorium, the Man in Black enjoyed a heightened national profile. The year before, he had recorded with Bob Dylan, released a second popular prison album, and scored the pop-crossover hit "A Boy Named Sue." He took seriously his role as an entertainer at a time of social unrest. "Till we start to make a move to make a few things right," he would vow, "you'll never see me wear a suit of white."

With his band—guitarist Luther Perkins, bassist Marshall Grant, and drummer W. S. "Fluke" Holland (partially obscured)—supporting him, Johnny Cash prompted the "King of Country Music," Roy Acuff (at right with fiddle), and other Opry personnel to "get rhythm" during a Grand Ole Opry appearance on March 23, 1963. Two days later, Cash would enter a Nashville studio to record "Ring of Fire," written by Merle Kilgore and Cash's future wife, June Carter, and inspired, Carter said, by her passion for Cash.

outlaws, legendary folk heroes such as John Henry, coal miners, prisoners, and America's dispossessed, among them Native American war hero Ira Hayes.

In 1964 Cash appeared at the Newport Folk Festival, which also featured singer and songwriter Bob Dylan. The two would team up later for a recording of Dylan's "Girl from the North Country" and for an appearance on Cash's network television variety show, produced in Nashville from 1969 to 1971. Cash used the show to feature the Carter family and to give exposure to such artists as Joni Mitchell, Ray Charles, Ramblin' Jack Elliott, and Mickey Newbury, among many others.

Cash made his most famous recording on January 13, 1968. *Johnny Cash at Folsom Prison* included a rollicking, live rendition of "Folsom Prison Blues," prefaced by the singer's trademark introduction, "Hello, I'm Johnny Cash," and enlivened by the shouts and whistles of the prison audience.

In February 1969, repeating the formula, Cash went to San Quentin prison, north of San Francisco, to record. The concert included another original song, "San Quentin." When he sang "San Quentin, may you rot and burn in hell,"

the prisoners cheered lustily. A novelty tune from the same concert, "A Boy Named Sue," by author and songwriter Shel Silverstein, became the most successful single of Cash's career. The Country Music Association named it Single of the Year and Cash was voted Entertainer of the Year in 1969.

A talented writer himself, Cash championed others by recording their material, among them Dylan, Kris Kristofferson, Bruce Springsteen, Rodney Crowell, Nick Lowe, Tom Petty, Loudon Wainwright, Tom Waits, and Beck Hansen. On his TV show Cash performed Kristofferson's "Sunday Morning Coming Down," a song with special impact in light of Cash's own struggles with drug addiction. Later released as a single, the song became the CMA's Song of the Year in 1970.

Cash, Kristofferson, Willie Nelson, and Waylon Jennings banded together as the Highwaymen in 1985, and released three albums over the next ten years. Cash's work with producer Rick Rubin on the CDs *American Recordings* and *Unchained* recaptured the power of Cash's early sides with Phillips and earned him Grammy awards. In 2000 Cash assembled a three-CD compilation, gathering songs in collections titled *God, Love,* and *Murder.* Throughout, his voice conveys experience and authority: this is a man who has been places and seen things, and he knows things the listener wants to know.

JAY ORR

In this August 30, 1968, appearance, Johnny Cash appeared with Marshall Grant, Carl Perkins, and June, Anita, Maybelle, and Helen Carter. A month before, Cash had recorded Perkins' "Daddy Sang Bass" with the same lineup, supplemented by Luther Perkins, the Statler Brothers, and Jan Howard. The song became a No. 1 country hit. Like Cash, Carl Perkins came from poor farming stock, got his start in music at Sun Records, and struggled to overcome substance abuse. "Carl often befriended me and counseled me with a wisdom beyond his years," Cash once wrote.

A familiar part of any Hank Snow performance was likely to be a sparkling acoustic guitar solo, played by the singer himself. Most of his hit songs were also his own compositions.

HANK Snow

OF THE RELATIVELY few Canadian stars who have crossed over and made it in the "lower forty-eight," the best known is undoubtedly Hank Snow. Always elegant and neatly dressed in the best spangled Nudie suits, Hank emerged as one of the cornerstones of the classic country sound: for six decades he maintained his distinctive and unmistakable vocal style, his well-crafted songs, and his superb acoustic guitar playing. His discography numbered over 840 commercial recordings, one of the largest in the music business. His songs like "I'm Movin' On," "I Don't Hurt Anymore," "I've Been Everywhere," and "Hello Love" have become the best of country standards, and his admirers have ranged from Elvis Presley to Willie Nelson.

Born Clarence Eugene Snow in the tiny windswept coastal village of Brooklyn in Nova Scotia, his life was a Dickensian story of poverty and abuse.

To escape a brutal stepfather, he went to sea as a teenager in a fishing trawler in the rough North Atlantic. (These experiences led him to later form a foundation for abused children.)

By 1933 Snow was singing over the radio in Halifax, doing Jimmie Rodgers songs and, in tribute to Rodgers, billing himself as "the Singing Ranger." Soon he had a contract with Canadian Bluebird, and from 1936 to 1948 recorded a long series of popular sides that were available only in Canada. After several tries, he finally succeeded in cracking the American market in 1948, and in 1950 his mentor Ernest Tubb got him a job on the Grand Ole Opry.

In the ensuing years, Snow demonstrated an impressive versatility. During those early days, Hank often traveled with his own rodeo and riding show that featured his trained horse Pawnee. The spectacular success of the self-penned

"I'm Movin' On" in 1950 led to a long string of *Billboard* hits; he was also one of the first country artists to use the LP album as an outlet for his creativity, and is credited with developing some of the earliest concept or theme albums. Hank was an exemplary guitar soloist, basing his work on that of Sons of the Pioneers guitarist Karl Farr. Snow's repertoire ranged from straight country to Hawaiian, cowboy, and vintage pop music, as well as recitations, gospel, and novelty songs.

When Hank Snow died in December 1999, friends around the world knew that an era had ended. "He was the great stylist," remembered his fellow Opry singer Jean Shepard. Others spoke of his creating a genre of his own—a genre called "the Hank Snow song." Given his distinctive style and huge discography, it wasn't that much of an exaggeration.

CHARLES WOLFE

At a party to celebrate the fiftieth anniversary of National Life, a young Hank Snow, who had just joined the show, performs with an early incarnation of the Rainbow Ranch Boys that includes Howard Watts on bass, Dale Potter on fiddle, and Hillous Butrum on guitar.

JIM Reeves

Jim Reeves moved from the Louisiana Hayride to the Grand Ole Opry in 1955. By the time of his death in an airplane crash nine years later, his warm baritone voice, smooth ballads, and ingratiating stage presence had made him world-famous and helped introduce country music to a wider audience. The Texas-born singer was especially popular in South Africa, where he starred in the 1963 film, *Kimberley Jim.*

JIM REEVES' RECORDINGS are an abiding reminder that country music doesn't have to be intensely emotional, sonically hard-edged, or rife with rural imagery to be great—it can be, in its own way, as cool and urbane as jazz. Indeed, Reeves routinely opted for the subdued over the gritty in his songs. In his most famous hit, "He'll Have to Go," he is as civilized in his conversation with his straying girl-friend as if he were discussing a fudge recipe. He doesn't accuse, demand, vilify, or even raise his radio-perfect voice. Clearly, it wasn't Reeves' dapper dress and regal bearing alone that earned him the title "Gentleman Jim."

Whatever his appeal, it has given Reeves phenomenal staying power. Of his eighty hits, thirty-four hit the charts after his death. During the twenty years following his death, he had at least one hit a year. Six of his eleven No. 1 singles were earned posthumously. In 1998, the aptly named The *Unforgettable Jim Reeves,* a collection compiled by Reader's Digest Music, was certified as having sold a million copies.

James Travis Reeves was born August 20, 1923, in Galloway, Texas, near the Louisiana border. He was drawn to music early and was singing regularly on a Shreveport, Louisiana, radio station before he entered his teens. Like so many others who would become country stars, Reeves was at first as attracted to sports as he was to music. During the mid-to-late '40s, he played minor league baseball until an injury in 1947 forced him out for good. After that, he turned to radio announcing while continuing to perform in his spare time.

In 1952, he signed with Abbott Records, a deal that yielded him a No. 1 hit, "Mexican Joe," the following year. This triumph led to a job announcing and performing on the *Louisiana Hayride.*

Jim Reeves patiently subjected his songs to what his wife called a long "incubation period" as a way of deciding which ones to record. But once in the studio, "Gentleman Jim" tended to be demanding.

Reeves scored five more hits on independent labels, including the No. 1 "Bimbo," before moving up to RCA Records and the Grand Ole Opry in 1955.

While Reeves ventured into standard country, novelty, and even folk tunes, he excelled at pop ballads that were fringed with choral harmonies, café piano, and occasional strings. Starting with "Four Walls" in 1957, Reeves made a number of forays onto the pop charts. In 1960, "He'll Have To Go," his biggest all-time hit, topped the country charts and made it all the way to the No. 2 spot on the pops. Always at the center, though, was that burnished baritone voice, radiating calm and self-control.

In addition to his recordings, Reeves took his music to the masses via several international tours and frequent appearances on network radio and television. He became a major star in South Africa and even made a movie, *Kimberley Jim*, there. A prolific songwriter, Reeves penned such hits for himself as "Yonder Comes a Sucker" (1955), "Am I Losing You" (1957, 1960), "I'm Gettin' Better" (1960), and "Is It Really Over" (1965).

On July 31, 1964, in Nashville, Jim Reeves died at the age of forty when the plane he was piloting crashed. Three years later, he was inducted into the Country Music Hall of Fame. Because his widow, Mary, had accumulated a sizable collection of his demo, promotional, and other unreleased recordings, RCA was able to enhance them electronically and dispense a steady stream of "new" material.

Interestingly, the label took a different tack in 1979 when it arranged for newcomer Deborah Allen to sing a series of "duets" with Reeves, three of which eventually charted in the Top Ten. But there was more to come. Emboldened by new recording technologies, Owen Bradley, who had produced Patsy Cline, and Chet Atkins, who had produced Reeves, paired the two dead stars on songs they had both recorded—but separately. This ghostly undertaking racked up two more chart singles in 1981 and 1982.

With the charting of "The Jim Reeves Medley" (1983) and "The Image Of Me" (1984), Reeves' days as a radio artist apparently came to an end. But his eternally repackaged albums continue to sell.

EDWARD MORRIS

Among the chief joys of Jim Reeves' short life were his wife, Mary (below); his first No. 1 hit, the 1953 novelty tune "Mexican Joe"; and his dog, Cheyenne (left). The faithful collie is buried under his own tombstone at the Jim Reeves Memorial Park near Carthage, Texas.

Ira (left) and Charlie (right) Louvin look over a song list with their longtime producer and A & R man Ken Nelson. It was Nelson who oversaw the development of Capitol Records' country catalogue in the '50s and persuaded the brothers to switch from an all-gospel format and try some secular country—with dramatic results.

The LOUVIN Brothers

DURING THE '50S, when the smooth crooning sounds of Eddy Arnold, Red Foley, and George Morgan were busy moving country music in the direction of pop, two young men from Henegar, Alabama, brought back to the Opry stage the high, hard harmony of an earlier era, and electrified audiences with songs like "When I Stop Dreaming" and "The Knoxville Girl." Their style of singing didn't come out of the movie studios of Hollywood or the polite radio culture of Chicago; it came from the deep folk roots of southern gospel music.

Charlie and Ira Louvin grew up on the vast, brooding plateau of Sand Mountain in northern Alabama, one of the last bastions of the old shape-note sacred harp church singing. In later years, Charlie Louvin recalled, "If anyone wants to hear where the Louvin Brothers' harmony came from, all they have to do is listen to a session of sacred harp singing."

Though they grew up listening to classic country duets like the Blue Sky Boys, the Delmore Brothers, and the Monroe Brothers, by the time the Louvins decided to go out on their own in the 1940s, that style was passé. They turned to gospel music, and made their first real mark by playing with Smilin' Eddie Hill over Memphis radio. Ira, the tenor singer and mandolin player, was the songwriter—probably the most gifted and versatile that modern Nashville ever saw. In Memphis the brothers introduced songs that would later become Louvin favorites, including "Are You Afraid to Die" and "Love and Wealth."

An early record contract with MGM led nowhere and the brothers for a time decided to quit music; a new contract with Capitol gave them a new lease on life, and in 1955 they were asked to join the Opry. Their Capitol boss, Ken Nelson, persuaded them to drop their exclusively gospel approach and expand into mainstream country. Soon they were saving their gospel sides for albums, and concentrating on singles like "Cash on the Barrelhead" and "I Don't Believe You've Met My Baby."

In 1964 the Louvins split up because of increasing personal conflicts between them, and each started a solo career. Charlie's led to a long string of hit singles like "See the Big Man Cry"; Ira's was cut short by his death in a grinding auto crash in Missouri in 1965.

Later stars like Gram Parsons and Emmylou Harris have kept the Louvin songs alive for new generations, and Louvin records still echo from modern CD players. For many, they have become the standard for country harmony. "Every time I need a shot of heaven," says contemporary star Marty Stuart, "I go an' listen to the Louvin Brothers."

CHARLES WOLFE

There was nothing soft or subtle about the Louvin Brothers' harmony singing. It was full-throat, all-out, top-of-the-range, hardcore Alabama harmony, and few could match the high tenor work of Ira. At times, his fervor resembled that of an evangelical Pentecostal preacher—a calling he had often considered.

Legends of Classic Country
1960s

In terms of the changes it encompassed and its impact on the future of country music, the 1960s was a decade that seemed to last a lot longer than a mere ten years. During this period, some of modern country's most gifted and influential artists emerged from obscurity and made their enduring marks. And in a larger context, it was during this period that the music took some of its boldest leaps forward in what had previously been a gradual evolution, more or less finalizing its transition from a predominantly rural and regional phenomenon to a commercial art form created and marketed with a national audience in mind.

Central to this regional-to-national evolution was television, which had become a nearly ubiquitous portal into millions of living rooms across America by the early '60s. Prime-time network and nationally syndicated variety

Merle Haggard (opposite) poses here with his band, the Strangers in September 1966. This former San Quentin inmate and Buck Owens protégé emerged from obscurity in the Bakersfield, California, country music scene to become one of the most influential and innovative singers, songwriters, and bandleaders in modern country music history, perhaps second only to Hank Williams in his impact.

Grandpa Jones, Minnie Pearl, Faron Young, Bill Monroe, and Patsy Cline hold up the keys to the city on the steps of New York City Hall on November 11, 1961. During the '60s, Nashville's record-making industry began consciously reaching out to a more sophisticated audience by "de-twanging" the traditional country sound and eagerly embracing uptown pop music influences. June Carter Cash, Johnny Cash, and Carl Perkins, opposite, perform together at the Folk Festival in Newport, Rhode Island, in 1969.

shows like *The Johnny Cash Show* and *The Porter Wagoner Show* did much to position country music in the forefront of the national consciousness—as did the wildly popular musical comedy *Hee Haw*.

Throughout the '60s, the Nashville music industry was largely dominated by a handful of producers and executives who had their own resolute visions of how country music should sound and where it should go. They were cognizant of the music's rising national profile and anxious to capitalize on it as best they knew how.

Foremost among these were RCA executive Chet Atkins, Decca Records honcho Owen Bradley, and, later, Billy Sherrill at Epic Records. Atkins and Bradley are generally acknowledged as the master architects of a sweeping musical trend that pervaded mainstream country during the '60s—a trend that Sherrill later embellished and aggrandized. It came to be known as the "Nashville Sound" and was heralded by some, damned by others.

The Nashville Sound was born of a calculated attempt to appeal to the massive country-to-pop "crossover" audience, an audience that was not particularly attuned to the rough-hewn twang and strident quality of hardcore or traditional country music. The Nashville Sound, for better or worse, managed to de-twang country by replacing the drawling vocals,

whining fiddles, and steel guitars with lush, urbane productions that often included pop-flavored choral arrangements and orchestral strings.

Some artists, notably the great Patsy Cline and the smooth but soulful-singing Marty Robbins, not only adapted but flourished within the context of the Nashville Sound. On the other hand, many traditional country artists abhorred its refinements as a bastardization of the music they loved.

As ubiquitous as the Nashville Sound seemed to be on record, it was only one perspective of the overall musical picture. The decade also saw some of modern country's most down-home, tradition-conscious artists like Loretta Lynn, Tammy Wynette, George Jones, and Conway Twitty rise to the fore—often while working with the very same producers who had ushered in the Nashville Sound.

Meanwhile, another unlikely musical movement was sweeping through the popular culture, a movement that would have a telling and salubrious effect on country: the national folk music boom, which was well under way by the early '60s.

The folk revival was embraced by major country artists like Johnny Cash, whose ambitious body of work encompassed all manner of Americana and

often addressed the same social and political issues as neo-folk music. In turn, the largely urban-based folk movement reached out into the hinterlands and embraced bluegrass pioneers like Bill Monroe, Lester Flatt and Earl Scruggs, and Ralph and Carter Stanley. While Nashville's increasingly polished mainstream had been giving short shrift to the leading practitioners of this stridently down-home musical style, the urban folkies extolled these artists for what they were: authentic masters of a unique grassroots American musical form. It was in bluegrass music that hippies and hillbillies alike would ultimately find common ground.

Yet the folk revival was only one of an array of musical forces that, despite coming from far afield of Nashville, wrought major changes in '60s country music and introduced a huge, new, youthful audience to the music. Two of the era's most talented artists, Buck Owens and Merle Haggard, came of age in the vital musical melting pot of Southern California.

By the '60s, both Los Angeles and Bakersfield, an agricultural capital to the northeast, were home to thriving communities of talented country musicians. These for the most part were the sons and daughters of the thousands of Dust Bowl refugees who had streamed into the Golden State from Oklahoma, Texas, and

elsewhere in earlier decades, bringing their musical traditions along with them.

Times were changing in country music. When an artist like Bob Dylan shared the stage (and the same social consciousness) with Cash and made pilgrimages to Nashville to record, and when Buck Owens and the Beatles covered each other's material, the boundary between country and rock was starting to disappear. The top country acts of the '60s transcended the times, and became a creative bedrock that still inspires today's innovators and iconoclasts.

Treading in Owens' and Haggard's footsteps, another influential nexus of Southern California musicians would come of age and find their distinct

musical voices during the later years of the '60s. Talented bands like the Byrds, the Flying Burrito Brothers, Poco, the Eagles, and the Nitty Gritty Dirt Band would freely meld country and honky-tonk influences with the more raucous and high-energy, cutting-edge spirit of '70s rock. The influential genre that they launched was a hybrid called country-rock. It not only captivated the Woodstock generation's fancy, but also influenced country musicians like Waylon Jennings and Emmylou Harris, whose impact would be felt in times yet to come.

BOB ALLEN

PATSY Cline

PATSY CLINE WAS elected to the Country Music Hall of Fame in 1973, ten years after her death in a tragic plane crash. The honor came on the strength of a recording career that had lasted less than eight years and included only 102 tracks.

For five of those years, from 1955 to 1960, she labored under a contract with Four Star Music that limited the material she was allowed to record. When the contract expired Cline signed with Decca, the label run by her progressive producer, Owen Bradley. At her first session under the new deal, in November 1960, she recorded "I Fall to Pieces," a quiet shuffle made distinctive by Hank Garland's ringing guitar, the Jordanaires' smooth harmonies, and Cline's measured but emotional vocal. The song went to No. 1 on the country chart and relaunched her stalled career.

Born Virginia Patterson Hensley in Winchester, Virginia, Cline started out singing for nightclubs, radio stations, and talent shows in the area. In 1954, she became a featured vocalist on Connie B. Gay's *Town & Country* TV broadcasts in Washington, D.C., and signed the Four Star contract. Her first single, "A Church, a Courtroom and Then Goodbye," was released in 1955.

From her earliest recordings, the basic elements of her vocal style were present—the brassy growls, the breaking notes, the tempo shifts, the powerfully sustained notes—but most of the material was mediocre. Cline sang in a full, round voice, not with the nasal twang of Kitty Wells. For over a year, however, her recordings went nowhere. "I'm on a honky-tonk merry-go-round," she sang in June 1955, and the words turned out to be prophetic for a while.

Cline's first major break came when she made an appearance on Arthur Godfrey's *Talent Scouts* show, singing the

Introduced by Ernest Tubb, Patsy Cline made her first appearance on WSM's Grand Ole Opry in July 1955, performing "A Church, a Courtroom and Then Goodbye." By all accounts, audience response was polite but not much more. Cline moved to Nashville from her home in Winchester, Virginia, in 1959. After a number of guest appearances, she became a member of the Opry cast on January 9, 1960. She would go on to become one of the show's major stars and the first female country performer to headline her own touring shows.

Clad in cowgirl attire on the porch of her family's Winchester home in 1956, local favorite Patsy Cline had stars in her eyes to match the ones on her dress. Five years later, Nashville and the country music world were in the sway of her pioneering talent, which attracted the likes of Louisiana governor Jimmie Davis to visit her table during a WSM breakfast celebrating the Grand Ole Opry's November 1961 birthday.

bluesy "Walkin' After Midnight" for a national audience. The song went to No. 2 on the country charts and crossed over to No. 12 on the pop side. But attempts to follow up by couching her voice in a more pop-oriented setting—even going to New York to record—proved unsuccessful.

Cline's style—and Bradley's production—continued to evolve. "Hungry for Love," for instance, recorded in Nashville in 1957, found the Anita Kerr Singers supplying "doo-wahs," Grady Martin and Hank Garland playing rock-style guitar, and Bradley pounding staccato, repeated figures on the piano. Clearly, Elvis Presley's example loomed large as her handlers attempted to find a niche for Cline.

Once she signed with Decca, giving Bradley the freedom to record her in the way he saw fit, Cline blossomed into the talent the world would come to regard as the greatest female singer in country music history. Bradley and Cline recorded pop tunes, country classics, and new compositions from Nashville tunesmiths.

Cline overcame her aversion to ballads and eventually embraced the Nashville Sound that Bradley and others came up with as a way to capture an audience lost to the Presley-inspired popularity of rock and pop music. With Willie Nelson's "Crazy" or Don Gibson's "Sweet Dreams (of You)," her voice became a remarkable instrument, blending beautifully with the strings, backing voices, piano, guitar, and six-string electric bass to make a thoroughly convincing case for the feelings she poured into her songs. Cline inhabits her classics with sophistication and taste—subdued, passionate, or sassy, as befits the moment and the material.

"I Fall to Pieces," "Crazy," and Hank Cochran's "She's Got You" all became pop hits as well as country hits. But Cline's legacy extends beyond her recordings to the many women she influenced as country singers, among them Loretta Lynn, Jan Howard, Dottie West, Reba McEntire, k. d. lang, and Linda Ronstadt. When she died at age thirty, Patsy Cline had established the standard for those who would follow.

JAY ORR

A wind-blown Patsy Cline steps from a chartered plane to play at New York City's Carnegie Hall in November 1961. The foremost purveyor of the Nashville Sound, she also appeared at the Hollywood Bowl and on Dick Clark's *American Bandstand*.

George JONES

One day, when he was only eleven years old, George Jones realized where his future lay. On a whim, he got up on a corner shoeshine stand outside a Beaumont, Texas, arcade and started singing. Passersby began throwing coins, and two hours later, to his astonishment he had twenty-three dollars. "That was more money than I'd ever seen, and my young mind actually thought it was all the money in the world," he recalled years later. By the time Jones quit school at age thirteen, after failing the seventh grade, he was a familiar figure on Beaumont's streets.

GEORGE JONES IS one of the most imitated and influential singers of the past quarter century. His powerful, resolutely traditional vocal style has come to epitomize for many listeners exactly what the essence of pure, unadulterated country music is and was meant to be. As singer Waylon Jennings once observed, "If we could all sound the way we wanted, we'd all sound like George Jones."

Jones has often paid tribute to the three legends who most inspired his formative musical years: Hank Williams, Roy Acuff, and Lefty Frizzell. But it is the distinct "slip-note," clenched-teeth, honky-tonk mannerisms pioneered by fellow Texan Frizzell that Jones took to heart and gradually alchemized into his own definitive style.

What sets Jones apart from so many other honky-tonk singers cut from the same cloth is his remarkably supple voice, so full of twangy, note-bending, diphthong-twisting textures and nuances. At his best, he is capable of summoning up emotions so raw, anguished, and profound that they are almost frightening. He may well be the best pure country singer who ever lived.

Throughout his career, the hard-drinking, fast-living, spendthrift singer had often dangerously blurred the lines between the heartaches he sang about and the hard times he lived—a quality that has merely served to enhance his musical credibility and sincerity.

Jones began his career as a Texas barroom singer, and, in many ways, has never really strayed far from that venue. The son of a hard-drinking sawmill worker and itinerant laborer, Jones grew up in a government-subsidized housing project in Beaumont, Texas, where he sang on street corners for spare change. Jones made his radio debut on KTXJ in Jasper, Texas, in the late '40s.

From a flat-topped, quintessential Texas honky-tonk singer of the '60s, George Jones not only matured into the silver-haired king of sad country "heart" songs, but, by the '90s, became a living legend. Fans have long revered him as the embodiment of all that genuine country music was ever meant to be.

After cutting his first record, "Ain't No Money in This Deal," in a makeshift Beaumont-area home studio in 1954, Jones hooked up with Harold "Pappy" Daily, co-founder of Houston-based Starday Records. Having scoring his first chart hits—"Why Baby Why," "What Am I Worth," and "White Lightning"—on Starday, Jones moved on to Mercury, United Artists, and later Epic Records. But the crusty, tight-fisted Pappy Daily would remain his manager and producer for many years.

Jones' earliest hits were upbeat and rockabilly-tinged. But he soon began to discover his niche and widen his commercial appeal in the early '60s with ballads of heartbreak and woe, such as his self-penned "The Window Up Above" and "She Thinks I Still Care."

But it was on Epic Records, working with celebrated "Wall of Sound" producer Billy Sherrill, that Jones really began hitting his stride and matured from a mercurial honky-tonker into one of country's most soulful balladeers with such '70s classics as "The Grand Tour," "These Days I Barely Get By," and "Once You've Had the Best."

Jones' 1968 marriage to country star Tammy Wynette—who, at the time, had already achieved her own success—not only raised his public profile, but also made his numerous personal misadventures fodder for the tabloids. The string of hit duets that Jones and Wynette recorded before and even after their 1975 divorce—"We're Gonna Hold On," "Golden Ring," and "Near You"—still stand as country music's all-time most popular husband-and-wife duets.

Ironically, it was in the troubled years after his parting from Wynette—during which he was beset by legal and financial problems, as well as by drug and alcohol addiction—that he achieved almost mythical status among country and rock music fans alike. In 1980, "He Stopped Loving Her Today," a mournful ballad of grief and sorrow that reflected his own turmoil, earned Jones his first platinum album, as well as a Grammy award. Two consecutive Country Music Association Male Vocalist of the Year awards soon followed. And Jones, almost in spite of himself, was a superstar.

During the '80s, despite persistent personal problems, Jones stayed on a roll with memorable hits like "Who's Gonna Fill Their Shoes," "Yesterday's Wine" (with Merle Haggard), and "Tennessee Whiskey" (with Ray Charles and legendary guitarist Chet Atkins). The '90s yielded more chart successes with "I Don't Need No Rockin' Chair" and "Choices."

As country music moves into the new century, George Jones has remarkably continued to record and tour, long after most of his contemporaries have either gone to pasture or faded into memory.

BOB ALLEN

George Jones became a country music singer in the '60s. His songs reflected his rural past as well as the hardships and suffering he endured—personal feelings he communicated best at such live dates as the early '60s New Braunfels, Texas, appearance shown below.

MARTY
Robbins

Marty Robbins attributed his enduring fascination for writing and singing about the Old West to his grandfather, "Texas Bob" Heckle. "He was a Texas Ranger and a drummer boy in the Civil War—or so he told me," Robbins recalled. "He sold patent medicine, he wrote two little books of poetry, he was a real storyteller. He died when I was six, but I remember him well."

THERE HAVE BEEN many distinctive singers in country music, but Marty Robbins arguably had the purest voice of them all, combining the silkiness of a '50s crooner with the soulfulness of a dyed-in-the-wool balladeer.

It was Robbins' marvelous voice and songwriting that enabled him to roam so freely and with such mastery from Hawaiian music to rockabilly to pop to gospel to western songs. During the course of his celebrated three-decade recording career, he became one of modern country's most beloved figures. In fact, a 1964 Gallup Poll named Robbins—who was then a ten-year member of the Grand Ole Opry, an avid NASCAR racer, an occasional film and television actor, and the author of a western novel called *The Small Man*—one of America's most admired men.

Born into very modest circumstances in the desert just outside Glendale, Arizona, Robbins came along a couple of generations too late for the dusty trail roundups and brutal cow town shootouts that he sang about with such fervor. But he was fascinated by the stories he heard from his grandfather, "Texas Bob" Heckle, a traveling medicine man, and he fell deeply under the spell of Gene Autry movies as a boy.

That may be why the versatile singer-songwriter (who had sixteen No. 1 hits and nearly a hundred chart singles between 1952 and the early '80s) is most often remembered for his abiding love and affinity for writing and singing songs about the Old West.

Nobody—before or since—has sung them better. "El Paso," a hit single from Robbins' classic 1959 album, *Gunfighter Ballads and Trail Songs*, reached the top of both the country and pop charts and earned the first Grammy award ever bestowed in the country category. "The

Robbins enjoyed driving "micro-midget" race cars before later graduating to thrills and spills on the NASCAR circuit. Despite more than his share of high-speed crashes, stitches, and broken bones, as well as two heart attacks, he called racing "an addiction."

Hanging Tree," a ballad he recorded with the Ray Conniff Singers for the 1959 film of the same title starring Gary Cooper, was a minor pop hit. So was "Ballad of the Alamo," which he recorded for the movie *The Alamo,* starring John Wayne, in 1960. "Big Iron," a somber, fatalistic gunfighter ballad, reached the Top Five on the country charts that same year. A sequel to "El Paso"—called "El Paso City"—was released more than a decade after the original and topped the country charts.

Yet even Robbins' earliest recordings reveal a chameleon-like quality that enabled him to glide effortlessly from rockabilly to country to pop-flavored teenage balladry. His "Singing the Blues" and "A White Sport Coat (and a Pink Carnation)" were two of the biggest jukebox hits of the mid-'50s.

Later musical explorations led to *Marty After Midnight,* an inspired 1962 collection of Tony Bennett–style pop and jazz songs. And during the late '50s and early '60s he even delved into Hawaiian music with a pair of popular album releases—*Songs of the Islands* (1957) and *Hawaii's Calling Me* (1963).

Robbins was second to none when it came to an evocative country ballad— whether it was a perennial favorite like "Devil Woman," his haunting adaptation of Gordon Lightfoot's "Ribbon of Darkness," or "My Woman, My Woman, My Wife."

Two heart attacks and open heart surgery in 1969 did little to diminish Robbins' incredible vitality and creative energy. His chart successes had waned somewhat by the late '70s. Yet he scored two final Top Ten country hits, was still turning in electrifying performances at the Grand Ole Opry, and was even competing in occasional NASCAR races, right up to within a few months of his sudden death from a third heart attack, at age fifty-seven—not long after he was inducted into the Country Music Hall of Fame in 1982.

BOB ALLEN

Though he was a religious man, as a performer Robbins balanced lighthearted tomfoolery with an earnest, inward intensity that fans found just as endearing. A few years before his death at age fifty-seven, he was asked if his chronic heart troubles, despite a physically active, teetotaling lifestyle, ever inspired self-pity. His answer was no. Reflecting on his many successes, Robbins replied, "I know a lot of things don't seem fair in life, but it all depends on how you believe. . . . My life has been a very exciting life. In my mind, I've just about done it all." Robbins, below, checks out his cover story in *The Cash Box.*

MERLE Haggard

CULTURAL OBSERVERS STUDYING the social history of America's working class in the second half of the twentieth century would do well to examine the music and career evolution of Merle Haggard. Rarely has a musician so accurately mirrored, and in turn been shaped by, his times.

In 1937, in the shadow of labor camps just outside Bakersfield, California, Merle Haggard was born to Oklahoma Dust Bowl refugees in a converted railroad boxcar. His father died when he was seven. Haggard's first career was as a petty criminal; several of his early hits ("Sing Me Back Home") concerned his life in prison.

Haggard also wrote and sang about blue-collar ("Workin' Man Blues") and family ("Mama Tried") life, and created stunning love songs ("Today I Started Loving You Again"). He tackled such ideas as pride and self-respect among people for whom the promised land

wasn't delivering. Early on, his songs developed a sense of loss—of values, of community—that continues today. His band, the Strangers, reflected the brooding side of Bakersfield honky-tonk, turning in punchy dance music but with haunting overtones; it included such architects of the Bakersfield style as crackling guitarist Roy Nichols and bristling steel-guitar picker Norm Hamlet. Haggard's vocals were heavily influenced by country's great postwar stylist, Texan Lefty Frizzell, but they also echoed California singers like Wynn Stewart, with whom Haggard briefly played bass.

Everything changed in 1969 when, with the nation polarized by the Vietnam war, Haggard hit with "Okie from Muskogee." Though it did reflect the outlook of a man who'd been given a second chance by the American system, he also seemed to mean it as somewhat of a joke, but the song provoked as much

Haggard has always been one of county music's most complex and enigmatic artists. He has tried on a remarkable number of personas and musical styles, often in direct contradiction to each other, and yet he's worn them all well. The man is always changing, and yet, at the core, always true to himself.

Haggard feels most at home when surrounded by musicians who, like him, know and respect the real deal. Porter Wagoner (standing left), whose recording studio Haggard used occasionally in the '70s, fit the bill.

bitterness as the issues it invoked (drugs, experimental sex, and antiwar activism). For the first time, Haggard became known outside country music. He was heralded as a symbol of the Silent Majority, and though he played into that image with another song ("The Fightin' Side of Me"), he quickly sought to show he was nobody's spokesman.

The work that followed was full of contradictions, as if he were thinking out loud with the lyrics of each new song; many reflect not so much his thoughts, but his struggle to pinpoint those thoughts. Haggard became the keeper of the country music flame, recording tribute albums to forefathers Jimmie Rodgers, Bob Wills, Hank Williams, and Frizzell, and exposing the work of classic writers like Cindy Walker. After the Wills album, Haggard integrated Texas Playboys alumni into the Strangers and improvised dynamic, freewheeling sets unlike anything since the heyday of western swing.

His new songs cast him as a modern-day troubadour/outsider, more in the Woody Guthrie tradition than that of a jingoistic patriot. *Someday We'll Look Back,* his first album after the patriotic anthems, re-explored his roots while wrestling with feelings of being trapped between the promise and the reality of his new status; these ideas culminated in his acoustic-sounding 1979 album *Serving 190 Proof,* a midlife-crisis product of what he called "male menopause." His love songs grew weary and disillusioned, peaking with the 1983 "That's the Way Love Goes," marking his divorce from singer (and third wife) Leona Williams.

Haggard dodged all attempts to pin him down, crying out repeatedly for nothing more than the right to be left alone while decrying the influence of alienating city life, the destruction of the environment, and mindless consumerism. Those are still his pet themes today, along with rambling songs that look back to simpler times.

As the millennium drew to a close, he was country's archetypal worried man, singing his worried song. Although no longer a star, so far as country radio is concerned, his influence is everywhere—among transitional modernists like George Strait and John Anderson, as well as Alan Jackson and Clint Black, stalwarts of country's '90s "youth movement." He's the main man of alt.-country favorites like Austin's Dale Watson and a whole school of "Americana" singer-songwriters, including Dave Alvin, who produced a Haggard tribute album featuring Dwight Yoakam, Lucinda Williams, John Doe, and others. Haggard's individuality and integrity make him as respected as any artist alive. So long as country songs are sung, Haggard's will be prominent among them.

John Morthland

Haggard remains one of country music's most prolific recording artists, having released scores of albums and more than 600 songs, some 250 of which are his own compositions. Thirty-eight of his songs have hit No. 1 on the charts.

Loretta LYNN

Loretta Lynn nearly always remained outwardly buoyant, despite a life that was haunted by an utterly impoverished childhood, an often loveless marriage, premature motherhood, emotional batterings, and business problems. Her art sprang directly out of that harsh reality, reaffirming country's roots in folk music while setting it in the modern world. Ultimately, she earned the last laugh on success.

LORETTA LYNN WASN'T country music's first female solo recording star; Patsy Cline, Kitty Wells, Skeeter Davis, and Jean Shepard, among others, preceded her. But sassy, saucy, spunky Loretta was the first to portray a strong-minded woman who could, if so inclined, stand independently of her man. Before Loretta, country had "girl singers" who swore devotion to their men through good times and bad (but mostly bad); after Loretta, country women stood increasingly on their own. She changed the music that much. In 1972, she became the first woman ever named the Country Music Association's Entertainer of the Year.

Certainly her life was the stuff of country songs. She was born in 1935 in Butcher Hollow, Kentucky, the second of what would ultimately be eight children, to Melvin and Clara Webb. Her father's wages as a coal miner barely allowed the family to survive from week to week in a log cabin in the tiny settlement reachable only by dirt walking trails, no roads.

Loretta was almost fourteen when she married the first man who ever courted her, Oliver V. "Doolittle" Lynn, a carousing former soldier also known as "Mooney" (because he moonshined). She became a mother at fourteen (and a grandmother at twenty-eight). By the time Loretta reached eighteen, she and Mooney were living in Washington state with four kids.

In the late '50s, Mooney pushed her out to perform in local honky-tonks, and in 1960 she scored a national hit on a tiny Canadian label. This led the Lynns to Nashville, where she joined the Wilburn Brothers show, began working with producer Owen Bradley, and enjoyed her first major-label success—with a song called "Success."

Though "Success" was a conventional Nashville record on which Loretta

From backwoods shack to antebellum mansion, Loretta, Mooney, and their kids stuck by southern family traditions, and she spoke for a generation of women. Several of her children followed her into show business.

sounded like a cross between Cline and Wells, she quickly found her own feisty voice. It helped that in her early days, she wrote most of her own multifaceted material, often inspired by her turbulent marriage to the philandering, hard-drinking Mooney.

In songs like the sardonic "Happy Birthday" and "Don't Come Home A'Drinkin' (with Lovin' on Your Mind)," she laid down the law to her man. In "You Ain't Woman Enough" and "Fist City," she read the riot act to the "other woman." In all of these, Loretta threatened to take matters into her own hands like no country woman before her.

In "I Know How" and "To Make a Man (Feel Like a Man)," she flaunted her womanly wiles. In "Wings Upon Your Horns," she used biblical imagery to condemn the man who took her virginity and then spurned her. In "You Wanna Give Me a Lift," she turns another man away before he can do the same.

"I Wanna Be Free" expressed a restlessness, confusion, and longing that grew more credible as Loretta began

having physical and emotional breakdowns onstage. "One's on the Way" so skillfully expressed the viewpoint of a beleaguered mid-America housewife that Loretta was embraced by feminists when it hit in the early '70s.

By then, she had stopped writing, after losing a lawsuit to the Wilburns over ownership of her original songs. Just before that, though, she'd penned a romanticized look back at her childhood called "Coal Miner's Daughter," which completed her rags-to-riches transformation into a country superstar. "I was borned a coal miner's daughter," she declared, her diction going well with her hard twang. The title phrase soon adorned her autobiography (the first country autobiography ever to reach the *New York Times* best-seller list), which in turn was made into a Academy Award–winning movie of the same name.

In Loretta's era, a country singer, male or female, couldn't get much bigger than that. She maintained considerable success well into the '80s, both on her own and through her classic duets with Conway Twitty. She was eventually swept from the charts by new generations of country women relying on their own versions of pride, tenacity, and outspokenness, but there's no doubt that it was Loretta Lynn who opened the door for them.

JOHN MORTHLAND

When not working, Loretta relaxes on her Tennessee dude ranch. She and Sissy Spacek became best friends when the latter hit the road with Lynn to study her moves and mannerisms before playing her in the movie *Coal Miner's Daughter*.

BUCK Owens

"I SHALL SING no song that is not a country song. I shall make no record that is not a country record. I refuse to be known as anything but a country singer. . . . Country music and country music fans have made me what I am today. And I shall not forget it."

That was Buck Owens' 1965 Pledge to Country Music, published in all the trade and fan magazines. And with the exception of an early rockabilly folly issued under the pseudonym Corky Jones and a few later singles like "Johnny B. Goode" and the ill-advised "Bridge Over Troubled Water," he was remarkably true to his credo.

Alvis Edgar "Buck" Owens might not have originated "the Bakersfield sound," but he became its poster boy and literally took it to the world. The Bakersfield sound was the music Nashville forgot, subtly warped and hardened in the isolation of the

California desert. It was steel guitars and blazing Fender Telecasters playing off each other, and drums to keep it dance-able. It was music that had migrated from Oklahoma, Texas, and Arkansas, kept alive as a statement about roots in the vast melting pot of southern California. It was hardscrabble music that was not going to slick itself up in search of pop airplay. And it became the foundation stone of alt. country.

Owens' pledge to country music came at a time when producers like Chet Atkins, Owen Bradley, and Don Law were in search of the middle ground where pop and country met. Ironically, Atkins, then heading RCA's country division, had the chance to sign Owens; Don Law at Columbia Records also came close to offering the singer a con-tract. Had Buck gone with either (or with Owen Bradley, for that matter), he might have been force-fed Nashville

With his trademark red, white, and blue guitar, Buck Owens was one of the most visible country stars of the '60s and '70s. Pensive and astute, he served a long apprenticeship before his breakthrough. His danceable, hard-driving sound, out of fashion for much of the '70s and '80s, eventually shaped the alt.-country movement of the '90s.

Much maligned for its hokiness and for reinforcing negative stereotypes, *Hee Haw* was nonetheless the most successful syndicated television show of all time, and Buck Owens, its host from 1969 to 1986, is still the performer most closely identified with it. *Hee Haw*'s success attracted the cream of country talent, and Owens is seen below seated at the far right with (left to right) Grandpa Jones, Minnie Pearl, and Roy Acuff.

songs and nudged toward the Nashville mainstream.

Instead, he was signed by Ken Nelson of Capitol Records, a hands-off producer whose creative latitude played an integral role in the development of Owens' artistry. Nelson let him record his own songs with his own band, drawing infrequently on the Nashville song mill. Nelson also let him make treble-heavy records that cut through the small, muddy sound of car radios.

Buck Owens was the complete package. He wrote songs, played lead guitar, and effectively produced his own records. Unfortunately, he came to Capitol in mid-1957, just as the rockabillies were dictating airplay, and had to wait two years for the pendulum to swing back. But in late 1959, when "Under Your Spell Again" hit No. 4 on *Billboard's* country listing, Owens' career took off, and nearly every one of his subsequent records reached the charts. His first No. 1 hit, "Act Naturally," was covered by the Beatles, and songs like "Together Again" and "I've Got a Tiger by the Tail" are unornamented and ageless.

In 1969, Owens brought his music to prime-time television on the much-maligned *Hee Haw*. From the time the show became successful, his releases were punctuated by novelty songs that went over well with viewers, like "Monster's Holiday" and "Made in Japan."

Things slowly unraveled for Buck Owens when his lead guitarist, Don Rich, who had begun his musical career with Owens at the age of sixteen, died suddenly in 1974. Further upset by "urban cowboy" pop-country, Owens

stopped recording in 1980 and retired to run his Bakersfield-based radio empire, traveling to Nashville twice a year to tape *Hee Haw*.

For several years, little was heard of him. He had always taken care of his business affairs, co-managing himself and publishing his own songs as well as most of Merle Haggard's early work. He had also written a clause into his 1971 Capitol contract renewal stating that all his masters would revert to him five years after expiration, and, in 1980, he became the first major country artist to assume control of his own catalog. The CD revolution around the corner made that acquisition a valuable asset.

Buck Owens might have remained gainfully unemployed had Dwight Yoakam, whose music was more or less Bakersfield nouveau, not coaxed him out of retirement. They formed a curious father-son type of act, topping the charts in 1988 with "Streets of Bakersfield." Owens' music passed via Yoakam into the alt.-country mainstream, its twangy sound now heard more often than at any time since the mid-'60s.

The Nashville-centric history of country music had a hard time allowing Owens the credit he is due, but the fact remains that he kept the honky-tonk roots of country music alive when Nashville saw them as an embarrassing throwback. His 1996 election to the Country Music Hall of Fame was tacit acknowledgment that he had been right all along.

COLIN ESCOTT

Unlike most of their Nashville counterparts, Buck Owens' Buckaroos played on his records and helped shape what is now one of the most influential sounds in country music. Owens' long-serving guitarist, Don Rich, is—appropriately enough—to his right. They worked together from 1958 until Rich's death in 1974.

TAMMY
Wynette

One of country's most glamorous ladies, Tammy Wynette was still, underneath, Wynette Pugh, a girl who grew up poor in the rural South. She tried to keep the two personalities separate. "Wynette Pugh was a scared little farm girl who got a high school education, married very young, and made a lot of mistakes," she said. "And then there's Tammy Wynette, who got most of her education on the road, learned how to work out problems, and be what the name Tammy Wynette implies—a singer—when I go out onstage."

THE PREMIERE PURVEYOR of woman-to-woman songs, Tammy Wynette forged her considerable reputation speaking to and for blue-collar housewives who ached for romantic release, if not "D-I-V-O-R-C-E."

Along with Loretta Lynn and Dolly Parton, the Mississippi-born Virginia Wynette Pugh defined female country music from the late '60s through the '70s. But while Lynn and Parton presented themselves through an amiable façade, Wynette never backed away from the dramatic, often tragic material of domestic torment, delivering her songs with a racking sob that conveyed a universe of suffering. Such pleas for love, fidelity, and forgiveness drew loyal appreciation from her mostly female fans, and sold more than thirty million records.

A bridge between old-style country and a younger generation that includes Lorrie Morgan, Reba McEntire, and Pam Tillis, Wynette sang of the blue-collar

lifestyle she knew in her youth. Growing up in the care of her grandparents, she picked cotton and worked as a waitress, a shoe-factory employee, and a beautician before coming to Nashville in 1966. There, hoping to place some of her original songs, she met the legendary producer Billy Sherrill.

Sherrill heard the limitations to her voice but recognized that her pinched, tense delivery conveyed a kind of ennobling sorrow unlike that of any other contemporary female. With the right material, he later remembered, this "pale, skinny little blond at her rope's end" could move out of a government housing project and into the psyches of millions of frustrated and lonely working-class women.

Together, starting with "Apartment #9," "Your Good Girl's Gonna Go Bad," and "I Don't Wanna Play House," which won a Grammy, Wynette and Sherrill

Alongside Dolly Parton and Loretta Lynn, Tammy Wynette, pictured here in 1977, dominated the country music charts in the '70s, bringing a new, uniquely female perspective to the genre. All three singer-songwriters drew on their difficult pasts to express themselves through song.

built an image of an outspoken woman who knew exactly what she wanted—and didn't want—from the opposite sex. In 1968, she recorded the back-to-back signature songs, "D-I-V-O-R-C-E" and "Stand By Your Man," which spoke volumes about female domestic strength, and examined the complex feelings of women facing the breakup of a family. "Stand By Your Man" drew hails of criticism in the burgeoning days of the women's liberation movement, but proved a tremendous hit, reaching No. 1 on the country charts and No. 19 on the pops charts.

Wynette herself stood by only one of her five husbands—George Richey—but the most celebrated was the great country crooner George Jones, her duet partner on numerous hit records such as "Golden Ring" and "(We're Not) The Jet Set." With their 1969 marriage, they became the "President and First Lady"—and one of the most famous duets—of country music, spawning a huge fan following that monitored every wave of their turbulent marriage until it ended in 1975.

As she made the transition from hit-maker to legend, Wynette tackled more challenging and diverse material, including a single with British dance rappers KLF, "Justified and Ancient," which went to No. 1 in eighteen countries in 1992. Other collaborations included 1993's *Honky-Tonk Angels*, with Dolly Parton and Loretta Lynn, and 1995's *Without Walls*, which featured duets with Aaron Neville, Sting, and Elton John. Her last album release was 1995's *One*, a collection of new duets with former husband George Jones.

Even as her music career wound to a close, Wynette was revered as a pioneer—her *Greatest Hits, Volume 1*, became the first album by a female country singer certified gold by the Recording Industry Association of America—and as an artist, her still-sobbing voice carrying a hint of barely contained tragedy. Long plagued by a barrage of health problems, she died at age fifty-five on April 6, 1998.

Throughout her career, and especially during her early honky-tonk phase and marriage to Jones, Tammy Wynette had recorded material that seemed to reflect her own life. It also mirrored the concerns of working mothers everywhere—parenting, keeping a job, and trying to hold a marriage together in the fray. In recognition of those and her many contributions to music, she was elected posthumously to the Country Music Hall of Fame in 1998.

ALANNA NASH

George Jones and Tammy Wynette's musical partnership took them to the top of the country charts three times— even while Jones' unconventional singing style made him a difficult duet partner. "He doesn't open his mouth a lot—he sings through his teeth," Wynette said. "But I've learned that when he dips his chin down, he's going for a low note, and when he slings his head back, he's going high."

Legends of Classic Country
1970s

The decade of the 1970s—particularly the first half—was a period of considerable upheaval in country music. It was a time when dramatic changes were taking place in American popular music sparked by the rise of the youthful, counter-cultural movement from the late '60s, which created a renaissance of candor, innovation, and political awareness in rock and folk music.

Inevitably these winds of change made themselves felt in Nashville's traditionally conservative and insular music industry. This new age was ushered in by a loosely knit, musically rebellious, underground community of artists and songwriters—self-styled "outsiders" in Nashville and elsewhere—whose highly personalized musical visions butted heads with Nashville's buttoned-down musical establishment.

Though her talents took her to Nashville, Hollywood, and beyond, Dolly Parton has returned repeatedly to her East Tennessee Smoky Mountain roots for inspiration as a songwriter and artist. Through the years, Parton has contributed heavily to worthy causes in her home county. In 1985 she opened Dollywood, a theme park that has not only contributed to the local economy but become one of the South's leading tourist attractions. The lawn of the Sevier County courthouse is even adorned with a life-size statue of the hometown girl made good.

Mississippi-born Charley Pride, below, is thus far the only black American to achieve enduring stardom in country music, scoring twenty-nine No. I singles between the late '60s and early '80s. Willie Nelson, opposite, appears at the Austin Opry House in Austin, Texas, in 1979. His album *Stardust,* released the year before, is widely considered one of his finest works artistically.

Willie Nelson and Waylon Jennings, who spearheaded this radical movement, made their presence felt in the late '60s. Eventually they came to be known, for better or worse, as the "Outlaws." Everything about the Outlaws—their long hair, Salvation Army–style wardrobes, freewheeling lifestyles, and willingness to incorporate the best and most unruly elements of both gutbucket hard country/honky-tonk and early '70s rock into their repertoires—made the Music City executives nervous. That is, until Jennings' and Nelson's records began topping the national best-seller lists in the mid-'70s.

At the same time, the '70s marked a coming of age for such stalwart artists as Dolly Parton, Charley Pride, Conway Twitty, and the vocal quartet the Statler Brothers. These artists flourished on the charts by reaffirming all of country music's best and most time-honored traditions.

As a centering counterweight to the extremes of Outlawry and traditionalism, the pop-country dialectic that had flourished in the '60s Nashville Sound gained fresh purchase in the '70s by way of mellow, middle-of-the-road crooners and smooth, purring singers like Charlie Rich, Kenny Rogers, Freddy Fender, Mac Davis, Anne Murray, and Crystal Gayle. On the other hand, artists like Bobby Bare and Don Williams drew thoughtfully on the topics of the day and the sleepy soulfulness of their neo-folk backgrounds to carve niches in '70s country's mainstream.

For all the decade's glory, the early '70s unfolded in Nashville with more of a discordant thud than a melodramatic bang. The nadir—and, you might say, the proverbial writing on the wall—came in 1974. That year the Country Music Association bestowed one of its top honors, the annual Female Vocalist of the Year Award, on urbane Australian warbler Olivia Newton-John, who, unfortunately, had only tenuous stylistic connections to country music.

The following year the industry, in yet another high-profile faux pas, again demonstrated how out of touch it had grown with its own roots. In 1975 the CMA handed its highest trophy, the annual Entertainer of the Year Award, to pop balladeer John Denver. By then, Music City's emphasis had shifted drastically from creating trends to merely chasing them.

It was right around then that the Outlaws rode to the rescue, exploding onto the charts with their tough, austere, and often openly rebellious sounds and styles, which were received like a breath of fresh air by country fans. A handful of these artists—Nelson, Jennings, David Allan Coe, Bobby Bare, and Kris Kristofferson among them—were soon embraced by the sort of huge, youthful, national audiences that the CMA could only dream of reaching.

Part and parcel of the spontaneous and highly personalized musical approach of the Outlaws was the blossoming of what has since come to be recognized as the golden age of the country singer-songwriter. While great country writers of the past had generally labored in semi-obscurity, leading '70s songwriters Kris Kristofferson, Tom T. Hall, Billy Joe Shaver, Mickey Newbury, Guy Clark, and John Prine became successful recording artists and, in some cases, stars in their own right.

These writers captured the public imagination by embracing influences as wide-ranging as the imagery of the nineteenth-century romantic poets to the folk and rock 'n' roll lyric surrealism of more uptown contemporaries Bob Dylan and Gordon Lightfoot. In the process, they not only injected a new layer of wit, irony, and literacy into the standard country song form; they also explored new levels of introspection and social awareness in the music.

Arising as fellow travelers alongside the Outlaws were early honky-tonk rockers Hank Williams Jr., Charlie Daniels, and Gary Stewart. Williams and Daniels in particular commandeered the country charts with a rough and rowdy country-rock sound that was closely akin to formative southern rock bands like Lynyrd Skynyrd and the Marshall Tucker Band, who, in many ways, were musical first cousins to the Outlaws.

And though Willie Nelson was at the forefront of the Outlaw movement, he was also the tip of the iceberg in an accompanying wave of talented Austin, Texas–based honky-tonkers, Texas swingers, and country-folkies Jerry Jeff Walker, Michael Martin Murphey, Steve Fromholz, Asleep at the Wheel, Alvin Crow, and Kinky Friedman, who rode the Outlaws' coattails to national notoriety.

The emergence of the Outlaws, Austinites, songwriters, and honky-tonk rockers marked, more than anything else, a rather drastic populist shift of creative control—the final say on song choices and production values—from a handful of often heavy-handed producer-executives like Chet Atkins, Owen Bradley, and Billy Sherrill to the artists themselves. The rise of these artists, as well as the parallel advent of such '70s neo-traditionalists as Parton, Pride, Twitty, and the Statler Brothers, meant that a lot of the old ways of making and marketing records in Nashville were turned on their heads. Mainstream country music, at least for a while, entered one of its most creative and adventurous periods.

Bob Allen

CONWAY Twitty

Conway Twitty, pictured here in August 1978, had an unlearnable sense of performance. His stripped-to-basics presentation involved no dialogue with his audience, allowing nothing to detract from the song. He was the master of the gospel-like slow burn, perhaps a legacy of the preaching career he once considered. High psychodrama characterized his songs, which were often short stories rendered in less than three minutes.

DURING CONWAY TWITTY'S last years, he must have reflected that country music had become very similar to rock 'n' roll as he remembered it: new faces, impossibly young and good-looking, coming and going so quickly. Twitty probably also knew that, in all likelihood, there would never be another career like his. Altogether, there were five decades with a Conway Twitty record somewhere on the charts.

For fans who live by statistics, Conway Twitty was the best-charting country star of the '70s, ran a close second in the '80s, and scored more No. 1 country hits than anyone else, in total nearly one hundred country hits and twenty pop hits, many self-composed.

Perhaps Twitty's greatest gift was his intuitive feel for his audience. Whether rockin' on *American Bandstand* or crooning in Branson, Conway Twitty knew his crowd. In the '50s and early '60s he was a rock star, a phase of his career encapsulated in one luminous moment, "It's Only Make Believe." Then, when rock changed in the mid-'60s, he realized that neither he nor his fans were listening. Country music spoke to him in a way that rock didn't, so he summoned the courage to change direction.

Despite all his years in the spotlight, we know remarkably little about Conway Twitty. He didn't do the industry schmooze and rarely gave interviews of any substance. Often, his accounts don't bear close scrutiny, leaving one wondering who he really was. It's part of Twitty folklore, for instance, that Harold Lloyd Jenkins looked through a road atlas and renamed himself for Conway, Arkansas, and Twitty, Texas. Nonsense, insisted his ex-manager, Don Seat. By Seat's account, Twitty's girlfriend had come up with the name "Conway Twitty" long before he ever met Harold Jenkins.

Conway Twitty was always at his best before an audience. From a shaking spree in England in 1959 to a heartfelt solo on *Nashville Now* in 1989, Twitty was a consummate groundbreaker. Many of his duets with Loretta Lynn were sexually charged playlets that took male-female interaction a step beyond anything ever heard in country music.

Twitty, he said, insisted that his stage name be Harold Lloyd. A small point, but, in its way, telling.

Even the conversion to country music, the defining moment of Twitty's career, wasn't quite as it seemed. To hear him tell it, he was at the top of his game as a rock star when he decided to move to Oklahoma and revert to country music. In truth, he was a fast-fading rock star, knocked out of contention by invading Brits. Even then, he couldn't quite let go of his past. Owen Bradley, who signed him to Decca Records as a country singer, recalls that Twitty tried to hedge his bets, suggesting that he record rock as Conway Twitty and country as Harold Lloyd or Harold Jenkins.

The fact remains, though, that during the spring of '65, he walked out halfway through a show at a kids' vacation spot, hired a steel guitarist, and began booking himself into nightclubs as a country singer at two hundred bucks a night. That took guts. No one even imagined such a transition was possible. In the years ahead, rockabillies would forsake rock 'n' roll in droves, declaring that they had always been country, but Twitty was the first.

Twitty's vision of country music was defiantly hardcore. Some were taking the music uptown with orchestras and choruses, and others, like Kris Kristofferson, were stretching the notion of what constituted a country song. But Twitty had a blue-collar look—pompadour, sideburns, sport shirt, no hair over the ears or Nehru jacket—and a blue-collar sound to match: no orchestras, no sitars, no long words. The tempo rarely strayed above medium-fast.

Twitty developed a line of "bedroom ballads," songs that said what many men wanted to say but couldn't, and what many women wanted to hear but didn't. "You've Never Been This Far Before" and "The Games That Daddies Play," to name just two, were suggestive enough to excite controversy without getting banned. The sexual frisson took on another dimension in the duets with Loretta Lynn. The high psychodrama of hits like "As Soon As I Hang Up the Phone" and "The Letter" led many to believe that they were indeed romantically involved.

Early in life, Conway Twitty had wanted to be a preacher. Like a preacher, he was of his audience, yet apart from it by virtue of his gift. Jerry Clower dubbed him "The High Priest of Country Music," which speaks volumes about his almost messianic appeal to his audience—an audience virtually ignored by the industry at large.

COLIN ESCOTT

On television in England, 1959, Conway Twitty was the consummate post-Elvis rock star, leading the way from rockabilly to power pop. In common with many performers of his generation, he scored one "career" hit, but found it hard to repeat. By the time he switched to country music in 1965, his future as a rock 'n' roller looked very uncertain.

The title of Waylon Jennings' 1973 album, *Lonesome, On'ry and Mean*, really captured his life at the top during his multi-platinum heyday on RCA Records in the late '70s and early '80s. The unease, tension, and elusiveness that Jennings often conveyed on-stage seemed only to add to his anti-heroic charisma. "If we fought for anything," he said of himself and his fellow Outlaws in later years, "it was the right to be ourselves and not be typecast."

WAYLON Jennings

As one of the most popular and darkly charismatic figures of the '60s and '70s, Waylon Jennings was—and is—a self-styled outsider and vividly inspired musical maverick who helped change the face and widen the emotional vocabulary of modern country music.

Jennings was born in the Texas Panhandle town of Littlefield in 1937. In the early '50s, while still a teenager, he played bass for Lubbock rock 'n' roll star Buddy Holly, who produced Jennings' earliest recordings.

In the early '60s, before migrating to Nashville, Jennings recorded a country-folk-flavored album for Los Angeles–based A&M Records. In 1965, he was signed to RCA's Nashville division by legendary guitarist-producer Chet Atkins.

Jennings made some headway on the country charts with traditional country laments, but he also embraced and recorded music from far beyond Nashville's narrow purview—pop songs like the Beatles' "Norwegian Wood" and Simon and Garfunkel's "Bridge Over Troubled Water." By the late '60s music critics across the board were starting to acknowledge Jennings' adventurousness.

It was also in the late '60s that Jennings began to overcome an array of personal and creative obstacles and seize control of his musical destiny. He insisted on the artistic freedom to produce his own records, choose his own material, and use his own road band in the studio—freedoms seldom encouraged in Nashville record making.

Along with his wife, Jessi Colter, and fellow nontraditionalists Willie Nelson and Tompall Glaser, Jennings rose to fame under the slightly misleading moniker of "Outlaw"—not for any serious brushes with the law, but for their long hair, freewheeling lifestyle, unorthodox approach to music making, and the 1976 album *Wanted! The Outlaws*.

Wanted quickly became the first country album to achieve platinum certification, turning Jennings and Nelson into household names and making them two of the most highly paid and sought-after entertainers in the nation. By then, Jennings' powers as a singer, songwriter, guitarist, and bandleader had come to full fruition with a string of best-selling albums and No. 1 singles. His 1979 *Greatest Hits* sold more than 4 million copies.

Reflecting on the process of musical self-discovery, Jennings insists he's always made music the only way he knows how. "I never went out to set a style of any kind, just to do it," he once noted. "It just came naturally, I guess, because I don't know anything about music. I just know about my music. I have to do it like I feel it."

Bob Allen

Buddy Holly has had a profound influence over Waylon Jennings: Jennings almost ended up on the plane that killed Holly, J. P. Richardson, and Ritchie Valens in 1959. The coin flip with Richardson that decided Jennings' fate has haunted him all these years. Holly's promising career was cut short after only a few years, while Jennings continues to perform three decades later.

DOLLY
Parton

"My biggest talent is being myself," Dolly Parton once said, and she's proven it. Growing up in the backwoods of East Tennessee, she practiced the magic of positive thinking, drawing on her religious faith to believe that anything was possible. From the time she was a child, she imagined herself a star, bewigged and bejeweled with rhinestones. "I remember Dolly," says one of her neighbors. "She'd get on the school bus and have that old guitar and pencil and paper, writin' songs. She was about sixteen, I reckon, and just sang all the while."

ONE OF THE most influential performers of the '60s and '70s, Dolly Parton created a remarkable canon of country music in her early, autobiographical songs, many of which celebrated, if not also mythologized, her east Tennessee upbringing and a rapidly vanishing rural lifestyle.

Possessing the face of an angel and the zeal of a tent-show evangelist, Parton is a mountain miracle, a world-class poet in an elaborate wig and stiletto heels. Her Monument Records debut, "Dumb Blonde" (1967), presented her both as a spunky backwoods hopeful—with an authentically country voice that melded little-girl whispers, gospel wailing, and bluegrass tonality—and as a woman unwilling to accept traditional female stereotypes.

Parton's move to RCA Records in 1967 coincided with her joining Porter Wagoner as the pompadoured singer's duet partner. This was her first big break, replacing Norma Jean in Wagoner's revue for his television and road shows. At RCA, Parton began to establish herself as a hillbilly savant, writing frank and intensely personal songs like "Coat of Many Colors" and the album *My Tennessee Mountain Home,* gleaned from her childhood.

At her most prolific, no topic seemed taboo, from whoring ("She Never Met a Man She Didn't Like") and sexual voyeurism ("If I Lose My Mind") to old-fashioned lust ("The Way I See You"). Such clear-eyed, evocative writing as "My Blue Ridge Mountain Boy," "Down from Dover," and "Jolene," born on the breath of her shimmering soprano, caught the attention of artists beyond the strict confines of the country milieu and further forged Parton's reputation as a songwriter.

As a duet team who recorded a series of albums apart from their television appearances, Wagoner and Parton,

Even as Dolly moved beyond the boundaries of country music in the late '70s, she remained a country girl at heart. "I will always be able to help country music in many ways," she said, "mostly by becoming as big as I can in the entertainment field. You talk about country music in a bad way, and that's like sayin' my momma is a whore!"

with their carefully constructed harmonies and believable romantic angst, took an artistic back seat to no other such duo in country music. But in 1974 Parton's fierce ambition led her away from Wagoner's show and his control of her records. "I Will Always Love You," Parton's final goodbye to Wagoner, became a No. 1 hit later that year.

In the late '70s, Parton embraced a country-pop style that moved her into the show business mainstream and mirrored her brief foray into Hollywood movies. With "Here You Come Again," "9 to 5," and "Islands in the Stream," a duet with Kenny Rogers, she helped facilitate country's infiltration into the suburbs. Such material signaled Parton's move from an impassioned, country-folk song crafter ("To Daddy") to a multimedia star with tremendous popular acclaim.

During the '80s and '90s, Parton segued from powerful ruminations on isolation and loss to duets with younger male singers Ricky Van Shelton and Vince Gill. Still, she found her true creative spark collaborating with other women, especially Linda Ronstadt and Emmylou Harris, beginning with 1987's platinum *Trio* album, which charted four hits and pointed to a new maturity in Parton's repertoire and performance, blending folk, country, and pop in an old-fashioned, acoustic groove.

Trio II, released twelve years later, framed its songs as stark emotional portraits. The trio again strayed beyond the country genre to create a startlingly hypnotic, organic blend, and reviews often singled out Parton's renewed dedi-

cation to artistic excellence. In 1993, *Honky Tonk Angels*, a different kind of trio album that revived the old-time, traditional country female sound of Kitty Wells, united Parton with Tammy Wynette and Loretta Lynn.

Yet it took 1998's *Hungry Again* to restore Parton to her full grandeur. In 1997, middle-aged, enjoying no radio success, and as she later said, "not knowing exactly what I should be doing in my musical career," she retreated to the Tennessee mountain cabin of her youth to "write like I was hungry again." The result was an album with the kind of authentic, fiery passion absent from her recordings for nearly three decades. Backed by the alt.-country band Shinola, Parton performed a deeply moving set of autobiographical songs with two interlocking themes: the pain of romantic rejection ("I Still Lost You") and reflections on life at the crossroads ("I Wanna Go Back There").

Hungry Again, with its return to rural roots, was the sound of an artist who'd found herself again. Parton proved that truth with her follow-up recording, 1999's *The Grass Is Blue*, an album on which she, like other country singers of the time, explored the bluegrass elements of her hardcore sound. The record delivered inspired writing and enlivened covers, but for Parton's longtime fans, the quality of the music, plus the A-team of accompanists and singers Sam Bush, Alison Krauss, and Patty Loveless, seemed to say that musically, at least, Parton had come home to stay.

ALANNA NASH

Whether performing on the Grand Ole Opry (1977), acting in movies with such stars as Burt Reynolds (*The Best Little Whorehouse in Texas*, 1982), or writing songs, Dolly is intent on exploring her potential to the fullest. "I am a gifted person," she says. "I am not necessarily great, but I think it would be wrong for me to not try to exercise what talent I have and do with it whatever I can."

Looking very much like children of the '70s, the Statlers began the decade by singing about the newfound nostalgia for the '50s. The Statlers' long-term success gave rise to the term "Statlerized" to describe their take on nostalgia and American values.

The STATLER Brothers

THOUGH THE STATLER Brothers are the best known modern country vocal group, and though they have had hit records of every type for four decades, many fans still tend to associate the Statler Brothers with one theme: nostalgia. They relate to the Statlers through songs such as "Class of '57," "Do You Remember These," and "Whatever Happened to Randolph Scott?" and with the idea that "the good old days" doesn't mean barbershop quartets and the old swimming hole, but the images of the '50s—bobby socks, big-finned Chevys, and knock-knock jokes.

Some cynics referred to the Statlers as the "Nostalgia Brothers" and accused them of using the '50s as their sales gimmick, but millions of enthusiastic fans saw beyond this to the group's superb musicianship, their song-writing ability, and their folksy-but-hip image. They agreed with novelist Kurt Vonnegut, who called them "America's poets" and

who suggested that "Class of '57" ought to "become our national anthem for a little while" because of its honest treatment of faded dreams. Like many other legends in country, the Statlers built their music on bedrock traditions—in their case, classic four-part harmony—but they decked it out in the styles and themes of the '70s and '80s.

Ironically, the Statler Brothers are not Statlers, nor are all of them even brothers. The name came from a box of tissues in a hotel room as the singers were casting about for a good name. "We might have just as easily been called the Kleenex Brothers," one of them joked. The real brothers were Harold and Don Reid, joined by childhood friends Lew DeWitt and Phil Balsley. All had grown up in the Shenandoah Valley town of Staunton, Virginia, and began by singing gospel music in area churches. In 1964 they were discovered by Johnny Cash and hired to

tour with his revue. Their hit "Flowers on the Wall," which Cash helped to arrange at Columbia, gave them the impetus to go out on their own.

The Statlers hit their stride in 1970, joined Mercury Records, and started working with producer Jerry Kennedy. "Bed of Roses" initiated a wave of hit singles, demonstrating their signature blend of simple melodies and mellow harmonies.

Tragedy struck in 1981 when DeWitt discovered he had contracted Crohn's disease and had to leave the group. After much anguish, the Statlers decided to carry on, and replaced DeWitt with Jimmy Fortune, whose sky-high tenor and song-writing ability helped propel the group into a second string of hits in the '80s. In 1991 their weekly television show premiered on the Nashville Network and quickly became the network's highest-rated show.

CHARLES WOLFE

The young Statler Brothers—Lew DeWitt, Don Reid, Harold Reid, and Phil Balsley—lay down their trademark harmonies at one of their very first recording sessions, for Columbia, in Nashville, on December 2, 1965.

Willie NELSON

SINCE THE MID-'70S, Willie Hugh Nelson has enjoyed a widespread appeal that has put him in a rarified category with other great American originals like Ray Charles and the late Frank Sinatra.

As a boy in rural central Texas, Nelson eagerly soaked up the myriad of musical influences he heard all around him—the honky-tonk music of fellow Texans Ernest Tubb and Lefty Frizzell, the gospel blues of the field hands with whom he occasionally picked cotton, the western swing of Bob Wills, even the oom-pah sounds of the German-American polka bands he played in as a teenager.

With his wiry, rustic baritone and distinct vocal phrasing—a penchant for singing either slightly behind or ahead of the beat, which he picked up listening to Frank Sinatra's records—Nelson effectively embraced and assimilated into his vast repertoire everything from gutbucket honky-tonk and western (cowboy) music

to Tin Pan Alley pop tunes of the '30s and '40s and even jazz and rural blues.

These influences, combined with an abiding fondness for American popular music in all its incarnations, has made Nelson one of the most versatile, prolific, and musically adventurous artists of the last quarter of the twentieth century.

Nelson was born in Abbott, Texas, in 1933. After a brief stint in the Air Force and as a country deejay, he began his music career in earnest, playing the rough-and-tumble clubs in and around Houston in the late '50s. Soon he was penning songs, like "Family Bible" and "Night Life" (later recorded by Ray Price and Frank Sinatra), that would eventually become American standards.

By the early '60s Nelson had moved to Nashville, where he earned a hefty income as one of the era's most successful country songwriters. "Crazy" (a hit for Patsy Cline), "Funny How Time Slips

Throughout the '80s and '90s, Willie Nelson earned a reputation as a social activist. The "Red Headed Stranger" was a tireless advocate for the American farmer. He not only participated in and helped organize numerous annual Farm Aid events, he even personally lobbied Capitol Hill on behalf of farmers. While devoting much time and energy to political causes, Nelson continued to perform, both as a musician and as a film actor.

Willie Nelson appeared at the Country Music Association Awards show in 1993. Fourteen years earlier at the same annual awards event, he won the CMA's top honor: the Entertainer of the Year Award. During the '60s, Nelson made occasional appearances like the one below on November 28, 1964, at Nashville's Grand Ole Opry. Though he had a few hits during the decade and immense success as a songwriter, even his best efforts to conform to the clean-cut, button-down mold of the prevailing Nashville Sound largely came to naught. His unique vocal style was generally misunderstood by well-intentioned producers like RCA's Chet Atkins.

Away" (first recorded by Billy Walker), and "Hello Walls" (a hit for Faron Young) are just a few of the many enduring compositions from his Nashville years.

Nelson embarked on his recording career in the early '60s and scored big right out of the starting gate with a pair of country Top Ten singles—"Touch Me" and "Willingly," a duet with Shirlie Collie, the second of his four wives. But with his unusual voice and unorthodox phrasing, he did not fit neatly into the staid Nashville studio system. Another thirteen years would pass before he made it back into the Top Ten.

His breakthrough came with a disarmingly austere but compelling 1975 album called *The Red Headed Stranger*. This conceptual song cycle was set in the Old West and spun a loosely told, almost mystical tale of love, betrayal, murder, and redemption. Recorded for about $20,000 in a Texas jingle studio, *The Red Headed Stranger* eventually sold over 2 million copies and transformed Nelson's status from an obscure, regional Texas singer to a national superstar and rugged counter-culture hero. It was this album that contained Nelson's first No. 1 hit, "Blue Eyes Crying in the Rain."

Around the same time Nelson's profile was raised further by the 1976 release of a compilation album, *Wanted! The Outlaws,* which also contained music by Nelson's longtime musical sidekick Waylon Jennings and others. It

became the first country album to achieve platinum certification for sales in excess of 1 million copies.

It's indicative of Nelson's uncanny ability to wear so many musical hats that he followed up on his heartfelt 1977 album, *To Lefty From Willie*, a tribute to Lefty Frizzell, with *Stardust*, a brilliant collection of classic pop and show tunes by the likes of George Gershwin, Irving Berlin, and Hoagy Carmichael. *Stardust* sold 4 million copies and remains one of his classic recordings.

In 1993, Nelson again demonstrated his musical versatility in an adventurous album called *The Borderline*, which included collaborations with Paul Simon, jazz musician Mose Allison, and Irish rocker Sinead O'Connor. That same year, Nelson was inducted into the Country Music Hall of Fame in recognition of his immense contributions to American popular music.

In recent years, Nelson has remained as prolific as ever. In 1998, he released *Teatro*, a critically acclaimed album featuring Emmylou Harris and produced by Daniel Lanois, renowned for his work with U2 and Bob Dylan. Since then, Nelson has issued an all-instrumental album and, most recently, *Milk Cow Blues*, a collection that spotlights such notable guests as B. B. King. Nelson also continues to tour almost incessantly, and once speculated that he'd probably get physically ill if he ever had to stop performing—though he's seldom stopped long enough to find out.

BOB ALLEN

Willie Nelson has produced a prodigious four-decades-and-still-counting body of recorded work whose cataloguing has defied all but the most determined discographers.

Charley Pride's stage shows are famous for conveying the warmth, intimacy, and sincerity that distinguish the best of his recorded work. Although Ray Charles has had occasional country hits, Pride remains country music's only black superstar.

Charley PRIDE

IN THEIR 1979 hit "How to Be a Country Star," the Statler Brothers offered would-be luminaries a wealth of "helpful" tips, the most memorable of which was "Get a gimmick like Charley Pride's got."

The Statler Brothers felt safe joking about the "gimmick" of race because they knew that it had nothing to do with advancing Pride's career. While America at large puzzled over matters of color, the supremely self-confident Pride just kept turning out hits. Between 1969 and 1983, he charted at least one No. 1 single each year.

Besides possessing a resonant, reassuring baritone voice, Pride was propelled toward stardom by his athletic good looks, congenial personality, and commanding stage presence. And he always knew the right songs to record. Usually they were love songs, and seldom were they angry or morose. There was never a chip visible on those broad, stylishly clad shoulders. Pride widened his stage appeal by choosing talented up-and-comers as his opening acts, among them Gary Stewart, Ronnie Milsap, and Sylvia.

The son of a sharecropper, Charley Frank Pride was born March 18, 1938, in Sledge, Mississippi. Initially, he was torn between sports and music. He bought his first guitar when he was fourteen and began playing baseball in the Negro American League at seventeen. After a two-year timeout for the army, he returned to baseball, finally winding up on a semipro team in Helena, Montana. Country stars Red Sovine and Red Foley heard him singing in Helena and suggested he come to Nashville.

Nashville music executives didn't quite know what to do with Pride—one wanted to rename him George Washington III—but they did recognize his talent. In 1965, Chet Atkins signed Pride to RCA Records. It wasn't until 1966, however, when "Just Between You And Me"—his third single and first charted record—went Top Ten that the label revealed his race.

Acknowledging such No. 1 powerhouses as "All I Have to Offer You Is Me," "(I'm So) Afraid of Losing You Again," and "Is Anybody Goin' to San Antone," the Country Music Association decreed Pride its entertainer of the year in 1971. That year and the next, he also won three Grammy awards. His 1971 recording of "Kiss an Angel Good Morning," another No. 1 country single, became a No. 21 pop hit as well.

In 2000, Pride became the first black elected to the Country Music Hall of Fame. Without gimmicks.

EDWARD MORRIS

Beaming with satisfaction and showmanship, the Pride of Sledge, Mississippi, waves his fans an affectionate farewell. Good Time Charley's got the crowd.

CREDITS
Contributors & Photography

BOB ALLEN is the author of *George Jones: The Life and Times of a Honky Tonk Legend* and of numerous entries in such reference works as *The Comprehensive Country Music Encyclopedia* and *The Encyclopedia of Country Music*. For many years, he was an editor-at-large with *Country Music Magazine*. His articles and reviews have appeared in *Esquire*, *Playboy*, the *Saturday Evening Post*, and the *Atlanta Journal*.

COLIN ESCOTT is a Nashville-based writer. His books include *Hank Williams*, *Good Rockin' Tonight: The Story of Sun Records*, and an anthology of collected journalism, *Tattooed on Their Tongues*. He won a Grammy for his work on *The Complete Hank Williams* (Mercury Records).

EDWARD MORRIS writes for Country.com, and is the former country music editor of *Billboard*. His books include *Garth Brooks: Platinum Cowboy* and *Edward Morris' Complete Guide to Country Music Videos*.

JOHN MORTHLAND has held staff positions at *Rolling Stone*, *Creem*, and *Country Music Magazine*, and is currently writer-at-large for *Texas Monthly*, as well as a freelance contributor to several other publications. He is the author of *The Best of Country Music*.

ALANNA NASH is the author of five books, including *Dolly Parton: The Early Years* and *Behind Closed Doors: Talking With the Legends of Country Music*. A freelance writer whose work has appeared in *Esquire*, *People*, *Entertainment Weekly*, and the *New York Times*, Nash has written about country music since 1975.

JAY ORR is the editor and senior music writer of Country.com. For ten years he has covered music for Nashville's daily newspapers, and his writing has appeared in numerous publications, including *Billboard*, the *Journal of Country Music*, *No Depression*, and the *Oxford American*.

RONNIE PUGH is a research assistant for the Country Music Foundation. He is the author of *Ernest Tubb: The Texas Troubadour*, and is currently working on a study of country music's political songs.

CHARLES WOLFE, a three-time Grammy nominee, is the author of some twenty books on country and folk music, including biographies of Leadbelly, Grandpa Jones, the Louvin Brothers, the Carter Family, and others. His most recent works are *A Good-Natured Riot: The Birth of the Grand Ole Opry* and the *Country Music Annual 2000*.

ALAN L. MAYOR: 94, 115b, 138a

AUTRY MUSEUM OF WESTERN HERITAGE, LOS ANGELES, CA, COURTESY OF AUTRY QUALIFIED INTEREST TRUST: 50–51

AUTRY MUSEUM OF WESTERN HERITAGE, LOS ANGELES, CA, COURTESY OF AUTRY QUALIFIED INTEREST TRUST/SHIRLEY TEMPLE BLACK: 51

BETH GWINN PHOTOGRAPHY: 122b, 142–143

FRANK DRIGGS COLLECTION: 10, 46b, 54, 55, 87

GRAND OLE OPRY ARCHIVES: 19a, 25, 27cd, 31b, 34, 35abc, 36, 41, 42, 43b, 52*, 58a*, 59*, 63c, 77, 80, 82b, 93, 97, 98, 100, 110b, 114, 124

GRAND OLE OPRY ARCHIVES/LES LEVERETT: 35c, 71a, 107a

HOPE POWELL PHOTOGRAPHY: back cover-c, 130, 132, 140

LES LEVERETT: front cover, back cover-bd, endsheets, 2–3, 27a*, 30, 31a*, 33*, 35d, 38–39*, 47, 58b, 60, 68*, 71c, 79bd, 86, 88, 90ab, 91, 95a, 99a*, 102ab, 103*, 106, 107bc*, 115a, 116, 118, 121*, 129, 131a, 134–135, 138c

LES LEVERETT COLLECTION: 6, 8, 15a, 17, 19c, 20, 22a, 23, 44, 60, 70, 74–75

LIBBY LEVERETT–CREW: 137*

MARTY STUART: 131b

MICHAEL OCHS ARCHIVES.COM: 84

RICK HENSON PHOTOGRAPHY: 119, 131c, 138b, 139

RONNIE PUGH: 27b

SHOWTIME MUSIC ARCHIVE: 1, 9, 11, 14, 15b, 18, 19b, 22bc, 26, 43ac, 46a, 48, 57, 62, 63b, 65, 66, 67, 71bd, 78, 79c, 82–83, 90c, 99b, 105, 108, 110a, 111, 113, 122ac, 123

SHOWTIME MUSIC ARCHIVE/BILL SMITT: 28

SHOWTIME MUSIC ARCHIVE/COLIN ESCOTT: 5, 63a, 79a, 95b

SHOWTIME MUSIC ARCHIVE/JIM DAWSON: 126–127

SHOWTIME MUSIC ARCHIVE/LYNN RUSSWURM: back cover-a, 12

SHOWTIME MUSIC ARCHIVE/ROBERT ELLIS: 72

*Image first time published